Celebrating
the Single Life

BOOKS BY THE AUTHOR

THE EMERGENT SELF (Co-author), 1968

THE PARTICIPANT SELF (Co-author), 1969

APPROACHING THE SACRED: AN INTRODUCTION TO SPIRITUAL READING, 1973

STEPS ALONG THE WAY: THE PATH OF SPIRITUAL READING, 1975

A PRACTICAL GUIDE TO SPIRITUAL READING, 1976

THE JOURNEY HOMEWARD: ON THE ROAD OF SPIRITUAL READING, 1977

TELL ME WHO I AM (Co-author), 1977

AM I LIVING A SPIRITUAL LIFE? (Co-author), 1978

RENEWED AT EACH AWAKENING, 1979

PRACTICING THE PRAYER OF PRESENCE (Co-author), 1980

CELEBRATING THE SINGLE LIFE, 1982

Susan Annette Muto

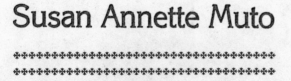

CELEBRATING THE SINGLE LIFE

*A Spirituality for
Single Persons in Today's World*

DOUBLEDAY & COMPANY, INC.
GARDEN CITY, NEW YORK
1982

Library of Congress Cataloging in Publication Data

Muto, Susan Annette.
  Celebrating the single life.

  Includes bibliographical references.
    1. Single people—Spiritual life. I. Title.
BV4596.S5M87   248.8'4
ISBN 0-385-18102-7   AACR2
Library of Congress Catalog Card Number: 81-43770

Contents

Preface

In contemporary society the vocation to the single life in the world is coming into its own at last. We have always had books and programs of formation for engaged couples, for the married, for clergy, religious and members of secular institutes. Most people recognized and encouraged these vocations. Ours has been a couple-oriented or community-oriented culture.

Where did that leave the single person? Often frustrated because he or she did not feel called to either marriage or community life in a religious congregation, secular institute or parish-diocesan establishment. Was it or was it not possible to live a joyful, dedicated single life in the world, fully present to self, others and God?

Despite the stereotypes and misunderstandings surrounding singleness, many people make up this important "minority." According to the 1980 U. S. Bureau of the Census report, the most significant recent developments pertaining to the status of the population fifteen years or older are the trends of remaining single (never-married) and the dissolution of marriage through divorce. The Bureau reports a rapid increase over the past decade in the percent of young men and women who have never married. For example, 50 percent of the women in the United States, aged twenty to twenty-four, were not yet married in 1980, as compared with 36 percent of the same group in 1970. While increasing proportions of the adult population are postponing marriage or never marrying at all, other persons who have married are ending their marriage in divorce. For example, in 1970 there were 47 divorced persons for every 1,000 married couples; in 1980 this number had risen to 100 per every 1,000 living within an intact marriage.

Persons living alone represented 23 percent of all households in 1980. Their number grew from 10.9 million in 1970 to 17.8 million in 1980. Most of this growth has been among divorced or never-married persons. Three times as many persons under thirty-five years of age lived alone in 1980 as in 1970 (4.8 million versus 1.4 million, to be exact). Although the increase in the number of persons living alone was not as dramatic for the older age groups, persons forty-five years old and over constituted 65 percent of the population living alone. Widowed persons constituted a larger proportion of all persons living alone than any other marital status category. At the time of this census, the majority of persons who lived alone were women (11 million women versus 6.8 million men). However, the number of men living alone increased by 92 percent between 1970 and 1980.

Despite these impressive and growing statistics, singles have often been denied a distinct identity. Many single women complain of being filed in the category of waiting-for-the-right-man-to-come-along. Other men and women are told, Maybe-God-will-still-call-you-to-the-convent-or-seminary. When these alternatives did not happen, single persons had to face the cultural stigma of being a "dried-up bachelor" or an "old maid/spinster/recluse."

This narrow mentality is coming to an end. Both Church and Society are recognizing what a powerful resource they have in single persons. Whether young or old, male or female, single by choice or circumstance, each has a unique opportunity to contribute to the well-being of our world. If statistics mean anything, we can see that collectively singles bring with them the idealism of the young, the experience of the mature, and the wisdom of the man or woman who has suffered much.

The aim of this book is to suggest, on the basis of lived experience, concrete, dynamic ways and means in which men and women are formed in this vocation to the single life as fully human, fully Christian people. Most of its contents are applicable to anyone who wants to live a seriously committed, spiritually grounded single life. Their formation as single persons enables them to participate in a special way in the transformation of self and world.

This book addresses especially single adults who have never married. Because their vocation frees them from the responsibilities of raising a family, they enjoy more opportunities for travel and leisure, more privacy and greater financial independence. Though the temptation is there to use these advantages—especially free time—for selfish reasons, it has been my experience that most single adults are altruistic. They care about others and they care what becomes of our world. But what they often need is a passing word of encouragement to put the creative powers of their minds and hearts into action. I hope this book offers that kind of encouragement.

Our approach is rooted in the basic or foundational spirituality that undergirds all human formation and that finds a privileged point of articulation in the Christian tradition. This tradition is further drawn out in many special expressions of the foundations as in the great schools of spirituality: the Benedictine, Franciscan, Dominican, Carmelite, Ignatian, Salesian and Spiritan, to name a few. Single persons, intent upon sustaining their vocation by deepening their spiritual life, may be attracted to elements of these special schools or even to elements of contemporary spiritual movements like the charismatic renewal. But, generally, in keeping with the broad-based nature of this vocation, single persons prefer a spirituality that gives them more direct access to the foundations of human and Christian formation as such. These foundations, once understood, can then be personalized according to each one's profession and position in society.

My experience has shown that the theoretical and practical implications of the science of formative spirituality touch profound chords in single persons' search for help in their spiritual formation. Perhaps this is so because of the presupposition held by formative spirituality that each of us is a single, unique creation made in the image and likeness of God. We are formed by God and for God from the beginning. This divine formation mystery permeates every fiber of our early and ongoing formation. Christian tradition teaches that this image of God, though veiled and weakened by the Fall, was not destroyed. The image remained, though the likeness was obscured. Our likeness to God is restored by Baptism through which Christ, the form of the Father, becomes the new life of the soul. We are transformed in His image by grace. As members of His household, we are called to the task of turning the world into the House of God. We follow this mission through the power of the Holy Spirit, who dwells within us.

In a concentrated way, the single person witnesses to this mystery of formation and transformation taking place in each baptized soul and in the world at large. He or she hears profoundly the message of Christ addressed through St. Paul to the singleness in each married, ordained or vowed celibate person: "You must give up your old way of life; you must put aside your old self, which gets corrupted by following illusory desires. Your mind must be renewed by a spiritual revolution so that you can put on the new self that has been created in God's way, in the goodness and holiness of the truth" (Ep. 4:22–24).[1]

This new self who is in all of us becomes the *raison d'être* of the single vocation. Singles must look for the why of their life in this mystery of being made in the form and likeness of God and in their call to manifest this mystery uniquely in life and world. God has some plan in mind for our lives when He does not give us a marriage partner or make us feel comfort-

---

[1] *The Jerusalem Bible* (Reader's Edition), General Editor, Alexander Jones (New York: Doubleday, 1966). All biblical references in my book are taken from this edition.

able with conventual or institutional living in a congre-
gational or diocesan setting. Given the grace of this vocation,
our question becomes: How can we as single persons grow
more gracious, joyful, open, receptive and relaxed about our
lives, avoiding all closed or defensive postures? How can we
witness here and now to the fullness of peace and joy toward
which God is drawing each of us in the age to come?

Let us begin our response with the bold assumption that
the single state is the foundation of all human formation. We
are born single (that is, unique) and we die single. In this
world, before one chooses any other state of life, he or she is
single. Only to the degree that persons accept this blessing of
uniqueness can they enjoy the togetherness offered by marriage or community membership. Married couples who really
love one another know how much the preservation of their
relationship depends on respect for their spouse's uniqueness.
Vowed religious agree that their solidarity as a community
finds its greatest resource in each one's solitude before God.
These vocations thus contain and value what Adrian van
Kaam calls the "celibate or single component."[2] God gives
many persons this original singleness or celibate moment as
their vocation. He calls them to give witness temporarily or
for a lifetime to the originating uniqueness that is His gift to
every human being.

In the chapters that follow I shall address these questions
and assumptions, trying as much as possible to relate my responses to personal experience and to root these reflections in
the knowledge and understanding provided by the science of
foundational human formation and its Christian articulation.

[2] Adrian van Kaam, "Family Formation and the Threefold Path,"
Studies in Formative Spirituality, II, 3 (November 1981), pp. 476–79.

Acknowledgments

Though this book is more an experiential reflection growing out of my own vocation to the single life than a scientific study, it draws heavily upon my life of research, teaching and writing within the Institute of Formative Spirituality at Duquesne University in Pittsburgh, Pennsylvania—an institute I happily serve as director and professor. Here, under the inspiring leadership of our Director Emeritus, Father Adrian van Kaam, C.S.Sp., Ph.D., the pioneering theorist in the science of foundational human formation (or formative spirituality), a group of devoted faculty, staff members and doctoral and master's students work together to unfold the principles and practices of this new field. The science itself touches every dimension of human and social presence and has a lasting effect on those of us who study its texts and participate in its courses, conferences, seminars and apostolic programs. My own contribution resides in developing the art and discipline of formative (spiritual) reading of both classical and contemporary masters of the formation tradition. The impact of such reading pervades many of my thoughts on a spirituality for singles, as shall become clear in the upcoming chapters.

My debt to the founder of this science, Father Adrian van Kaam, is greater than I could ever acknowledge here. His insights permeate each of the following chapters, and references to applicable sources will be given at the end of each section. I'll annotate these texts in case interested readers want to pursue them. I must also thank Father van Kaam for reading and generously editing the final draft of this book and for contributing the introduction.

Thanks must also be extended to fellow Institute faculty members, notably Father Richard Byrne, O.C.S.O., Ph.D., for his helpful suggestions on the text and welcome corrections.

Then, too, what would single life be without supportive family members and friends? I am grateful to my parents for their affirmation of this vocation and for their ongoing understanding of my personal life. To them, and to my brothers and their families, I can wholeheartedly say thanks for being kinsfolk and caring friends.

My gratitude goes out also to the members of the Domus Dei Corporation and its Imago Dei Association, with whom I share the apostolic extension of the science of formation to the general population and to Christian professionals.

Last, but not least, my thanks to the staff and graduate assistants of the Institute, especially Brother Romeo Bonsaint and Mr. David Nowak, who helped in researching and proofreading the manuscript, and to all those unnamed editors, friends and supporters who facilitated my bringing this book to published fruition.

Introduction

By Adrian van Kaam

This excellent book addresses mainly the solitary vocation in the world, a life that was especially lauded in the beginnings of Christianity. Many early Christians lived this call and were canonized after their death as martyrs, confessors or virgins. This vocation is distinct from the three other foundational vocations: marriage, clerical and conventual life.

The conventual vocation attracts singles who bind themselves under a religious rule in a community or hierarchical organization with shared obligations and with apostolic or contemplative aims. In this regard we prefer to replace the usual expression of "religious" or "community" life with the term "conventual." The common usage of these terms may suggest some underevaluation of the single or solitary vocation in the world. It may give the impression that the single life is necessarily less religious or less communal. Yet the single life in the world can be lived in union with God and in eminent service to society via the Christian pursuit of excellence in one's career or profession.

This book shows that neither the conventual nor the single life in and by themselves guarantee energetic, personal service of the human community. Both lazy and dedicated persons can be found among those called to any one of these formative styles of life. What must change is any underevaluation of the solitary life call, whether this is reflected in our language or in other overt or subtle manifestations of social injustice. Let me point out a few of the more obvious causes of such discrimination.

In its beginnings human society needed to assure the procreation of the race for its survival in an often hostile environment. The initial stress was on marriage as a societal duty to secure the future of humanity or the tribal or ethnic segment to which one belonged. Though such survival has been secured, it is still possible that the taboo against the solitary life as not serving physical procreation may exert an unconscious hold on humanity, especially in regard to women.

Operative also is the continuation of primitive forms of male dominance, implying that women are called primarily to serve males. From this narrow perspective, the female should be available to the male, if he so wishes. The possibility of a solitary life call for the female as a graced and beautiful option to be respected by all is the exact opposite of this male assumption of the availability of the female as mainly his ego-enhancer, servant or lust object. Normally, such primitive prejudices are not voiced directly but are symbolized indirectly in more or less virtuous-sounding phrases.

Another element that may have affected adversely the social and personal rights of singles can be found in the development of the clerical and conventual life from medieval times onward. In these options singles bind themselves to a more constricted style of community life and service in keeping with a special affinity of grace and nature. In medieval times these types of Christian communities gained enormous prestige, power and privileges. While such honors may have been well deserved, they led in some instances to the development of what we may call excessive security directives that were devised unconsciously to maintain this exclusive position.

One such device was the subtle intimation that a really generous and spiritual solitary person, not called to marriage, should join some particular clerical or conventual style of life, thus helping among other things to ensure the numbers necessary to maintain its power, influence and prestige.

A related area concerns economic social injustice. Until recently the free congenial following of their vocation was impossible for many single women due to institutionalized forms of social injustice. Society forced many women into marriage or the convent simply by making it impossible for them to earn a living wage and to serve the human community within a career of their own.

Not only the single but also the marital and conventual life may profit from the new freedom of women to follow their chosen vocation. The marriage or convent community may be less burdened by women called by God to the pursuit of professional excellence within the single life. Some of them may have been unconsciously compelled in the past by an unjust society to get married or to enter the convent as the only way of life for them.

I remember years ago in Holland joining the Life School Programs in mills and factories initiated by a Ms. Schouwenaars from Belgium. She lived her single life in service of underprivileged girls laboring in these factories, who had never had the benefit of formation and education beyond elementary school. With other dedicated professionals, we were able to persuade many company officials to allow the girls four hours a week off from their machines to engage in formation sessions that we conducted in the cafeterias of the mills during working hours.

One interesting feature of the program was that we never mentioned any of the traditionally lauded vocations without always praising explicitly the calling to the single life. In this way we hoped to serve the liberation of women for their own choice of a congenial style of formation in the face of institutionalized social injustice that had forced them for centuries to choose either convent or marriage, whether or not they were called to these particular styles of community service.

Ongoing congenial formation of one's life depends in great measure upon one's liberation from earlier unappraised directives. These are blindly adopted by us during the period of initial formation in childhood. More likely than not, at least some of these initial directives mirror the prejudices of our society. They were most likely accepted uncritically and communicated by parents and other significant formation models who by necessity dominate the process of initial formation.

If one is to appraise his or her possible vocation as single in the world, it is necessary to engage in a critical and creative reappraisal of possible prejudices. They mar the awareness of one's unique, natural and graced form affinity. It would be helpful in this regard to seek out formation programs that candidly promote such a reappraisal. By the same token, one ought to shun programs that prematurely orient everyone toward only one option, such as only marital or only clerical or conventual living.

Having gained this freedom from possible initial deformation, the person should strive for a sober and realistic understanding of the various options available to people today. The spiritual meaning and beauty of the solitary call should be affirmed as much as that of marital, clerical and conventual life. Subsequently, in prayerful presence to any one of these equally valuable options, we should grow to a decision, based on a clear insight into what each of these vocations entails.

Once one's call from God to the solitary life-style is clear, he or she ought to find, if possible, a support group of people. Single persons may profit greatly from periodic affirmation by companions called likewise to foster the kingdom of God by fidelity to singleness and its graced opportunities for the pursuit of excellence in one's career and profession in service of humanity.

As this book clearly demonstrates, the basis of any vocation is a profound human and graced affinity to the foundational style of life in which this vocation has to be realized. All distinguishing features of a vocation depend on this basic condition. Negatively, this means that the option for the solitary life in the world cannot be based exclusively on extrinsic reasons—for example, loss of a spouse, impossibility of finding a marriage partner or of being accepted into a clerical or conventual community, a desire to foster one's career or to be more free for travel, education or entertainment. It is possible that the Lord may use such initial extrinsic motivations as opportunities to disclose to people their intrinsic calling and affinity for the solitary life in Christ as an ideal of spiritual commitment in itself, not merely one valued because of such side benefits.

Positively, foundational affinity implies that one increasingly finds in this vocation peace, joy and intimacy with the Lord. A single person feels little or no envy, spite, jealousy, discontent or tension over the peace, joy and nearness to God that others enjoy in their marital or conventual life. On the contrary, such a person is at ease in affirming others in their calling and showing them the respect they deserve.

Another distinguishing feature of a true vocation is one's ability to live the single life not only joyfully, peacefully and prayerfully but also effectively. All of us want to participate effectively, within our limits, in the formation mystery that gives form to life, history, world and humanity. If we experience constantly that the formation attempts we engage in remain ineffective, we will face discouragement, loss of self-esteem, perhaps even despair.

We need, therefore, to experience a minimum of form-effectiveness to believe that our calling in some modest way participates in the formation mystery that makes life ultimately meaningful. One who lives a committed single life in the world must be able to set limited, realistic goals in regard to self-formation and formation of the world. These ambitions should enable the person to achieve at least a minimum realization of the goals that make one feel as if the solitary life has a good effect on the world.

This feature of singleness concerns one's ability to participate in some way both effectively and affectively in inter- and outerformation. Interformation refers to those relations and acts between people that foster their mutual formation. Persons called to the solitary life must be able to engage themselves as singles wholeheartedly, spontaneously and fruitfully in such interactions—without violating the limits of expression that safeguard their specific calling. A solitary person who constantly oversteps such boundaries or, on the contrary, morosely withdraws from any interformative presence, may not have a genuine vocation to this life.

Outerformation refers to one's forming presence to daily life situations and to the world at large as it announces itself in these situations. One is formed by these immediate and mediate situations while giving form to them in a unique way. If persons called to the solitary vocation constantly affect other people in the wrong way as a result of their singleness, or constantly refuse to care for them, we may again doubt the presence of a real call to this life.

In addition to stressing all of these features of singleness, *Celebrating the Single Life* highlights the uniqueness-element of God's plan for each human life. In many ways this is the main witness that the solitary life as a whole should give to humanity. People who tend to be absorbed in the pulsations of crowd and collectivity, without attention to the unique mystery of their own intimacy with God and His unique call of them, are probably not called to the specific witness of the solitary life in the world.

Furthermore, this book points out another distinguishing feature of this vocation: one's sensitivity for those caught in the circumstance of singleness without feeling able to opt for such a solitary life in the world as a lifelong commitment. In other words, there are those who may be single not by choice, but because of separation, divorce, loss of spouse, nonacceptance in the conventual life, or because of illness, old age, or not finding the right mate.

Persons, on the contrary, who are called to this life as a vocation to which they respond joyously by free option, on the basis of a true affinity, feel deeply the difference between their invigorating experience of singleness and the unwelcome experience it seems to be for those not graced with this calling. Hence, they are more sensitive than others would be to the suffering of people who did not opt for this life yet are forced to live it.

While involuntary singles may be unable to find the same strength and consolation in singleness as voluntary ones, they can profit from the wisdom, experience and commitment of those freely called to live this life. They can be helped by their words and example to see a deeper meaning in what they may experience as a deprivation and thus be encouraged to make the best of it. In some cases they may even find and accept a vocation to this life.

Persons called to the single life are invited by the Lord to maintain and protect this calling in humanity. It should be defended vigorously against social injustice. They must speak out when discrimination in any form is manifested. Single people should cultivate the gentle courage to withstand politely yet firmly any discrimination. For instance, their professional position may be threatened by unjust replacement by people less qualified than they are, mainly on the basis of the fact that the latter have had a clerical, conventual or marital formation.

Single persons should understand that social justice must be defended not only by words but also by deeds. In a case of discrimination against people called to the single life in office, factory, hospital, school, university or whatever, they should, as a threatened minority, help each other by legal funds too. They ought to support the legal battle against any demeaning of their call by colleagues and administrators who have chosen other life-styles.

In a practical vein this book treats several obstacles to effective single living. Many of these obstacles arise from the generosity and social concern of singles. The relative freedom characteristic of their vocation encourages singles to be socially present in a unique, self-giving and spontaneous way. By the same token, obstacles to the relaxed maintenance of such presence are abundant.

Social presence begins to erode and may finally be depleted if one's aspirations, anticipations and ambitions in the area of social care are exalted or unrealistic. Such exaltation seduces some single people to give in to others who demand of them all sorts of extra activities beyond their first obligation of effective social presence within their immediate profession and surroundings. We are only too familiar with the caricature of single persons involved in countless charities and apostolates who have no love, energy or time left to prepare their classes or publications well or to be socially present to their employees, fellow workers, administrators, colleagues or patients. They may think nothing of leaving their colleagues with the lion's share of daily work while they exhaust their own energy and dedication in extracurricular social activities.

Single persons caught in this bind are soon perceived as the ones others cannot count on either during or beyond regular working hours. They are likely to make excuses or protest if anything is changed in their appointment schedule. Sooner or later these types themselves begin to sense their own deficiency in everyday generosity. They may try to ward off this awareness by enumerating the many ways in which they give as much time and energy to the shared daily task as everyone else, but such defensive monologues mar their effective social presence even more.

Thus exaltation, in regard to extracurricular activities, unrooted in reality, can become a serious obstacle to the joyful and peaceful living of the single vocation. The daily task and environment must remain the arena in which singles first of all incarnate their single commitment and witness.

Both in and out of one's professional environment, it may happen that all kinds of well-intentioned people who do not understand the solitary vocation think nothing of imposing on singles as if they were their property. They usually do this by playing on false guilt feelings that appear to be awakened more easily in persons who remain single, a problem thoroughly addressed in this book.

Single persons are usually dedicated to service, but by the same token they may be inclined to stretch themselves too far, neglecting needed rest and recreation. Such deformative overextension leads to exhaustion or to what we may call social-presence erosion and depletion. Such eroding of social care harms in turn the formation of the spiritual life as a whole.

As this book suggests, if present trends continue, we will witness an increase in the population of singles. The continuation of a climate conducive to the single life depends on such factors as the economic freedom of women; the pluralistic nature of contemporary society, leading to diverse vocational choices; and mature appraisal by each person of the equal human and spiritual dignity of solitary, marital, conventual or clerical life.

Another favorable condition in this regard is the reemergence of certain comparable conditions of early Christianity where Roman decadence inspired single Christians to a solitary witness in the midst of a pagan world. The large population of singles, if maintained or increased in our time, may give rise in many to the disclosure of a vocation to live a similar life commitment of witness amidst what some diagnose as present-day narcissism. Many singles may discover a foundational affinity to this vocation as a religious commitment for life. Other Christians, compelled to live the single life temporarily or lastingly because of extrinsic reasons, may manifest an increasing need for formation models. Those single persons in their midst who have made the art and discipline of Christian solitary living a religious commitment for life, may be called upon to provide this model and direction.

Then, too, if present trends continue, Christianity will be confronted increasingly with other non-Western cultures and their paradigms of life formation. In the East, an awareness of non-Christian styles of spirituality is already unavoidable. Added to this new consciousness is the clamor of many for a spiritual formation that is basically Christian and not encumbered by accretions of special Western schools of formation developed by clericals and conventuals. All of these social-formative influences will serve to awaken a deep interest in a foundational Christian spirituality.

The spiritual needs of singles, combined with their tendency to reflection, will put them ahead of their time in this regard. Their commitment to the single life gives them, moreover, the freedom of time, space and energy to excel in such a foundational formative approach. As this book makes amply clear, we witness among singles an increasing concentration on the foundations of Christian formative spirituality and a desire to expand and deepen the nourishing spiritual grounds on which the solitary Christian life can prosper.

Those called to the single life do miss out on the beneficial, liberating constrictions of marital, clerical and conventual life, on their protection and forming power. Obedience to their own call exposes singles to many more dangers of distraction, self-seeking, sensuality and social-presence erosion. Yet, with God's grace, this call can be lived to the full in quiet fidelity to the foundations of the Christian formation tradition and the original spiritual experiences that gave rise to them.

The Christian churches of tomorrow may be in great need of Christians committed to the solitary life. Within the limits of their congeniality and in accordance with their other obligations, a number of them may make themselves available for services that are left vacant by the decrease in vocations to the clerical and conventual life.

The future development of the solitary vocation will probably lead to the establishment of support communities not bound to any specific religious community, secular institute or similar lay association in their distinctive spiritual or apostolic tradition. The main focus of the spirituality of single people, following upon what we have said, would be on foundational spiritual formation, not on one or another specific apostolic or charitable work.

Singles, supported in their vocation by such a group, would remain free to choose their mode of cultural participation. Such groups would be a whole new venture in Christianity, complementing the already existing variety of Chris-

tian communities, such as monastic orders, active congrega-
tions, secular institutes and similar lay associations. Then, too,
they would restore to life an important institution of early
Christianity, during which time solitary Christians were ex-
posed to the same temptations as their counterparts in the
modern secular world.

All in all, it is safe to say that persons committed to the
single life already play a major role in purifying and complementing the insights and customs that have shaped contemporary social and world formation. They have proven that it
is possible to live the single life in a normal, healthy, spiritual
and practical way without becoming odd, asocial or other-
worldly. I thus view this book as a major contribution to all
persons called by the Lord to bear the immense beauty and
burden of being solitary in the modern world. I also recommend it wholeheartedly to married persons, priests and religious seeking to understand and support their single friends,
colleagues and acquaintances.

1

✠✠✠✠✠✠✠✠✠✠✠✠✠✠✠✠✠✠✠✠
✠✠✠✠✠✠✠✠✠✠✠✠✠✠✠✠✠✠✠✠

Living a Single
Spiritual Life

Where have we come from in our understanding of singleness and where are we going? Are we right in our intuition that singles are seeking a spiritual life? We need to approach these questions from an historical perspective, for our comprehension and style of living the single life are rapidly changing.

Not too long ago, to be single was to be firmly bound to certain role models. A single woman was a "maiden aunt," a single man a "bachelor uncle." The place singles occupied in society was identifiable and secure, albeit a lesser place than that allotted to married couples. Even if singles were happy with their state of life, they were likely to hear such remarks as: "What a shame a lovely girl like you never found the right man," or, "Don't worry, dear, it's never too late." To remain a single person in the world required some courage. Especially in Church-related circles, not being married often left one on the defensive.

In such a case, people might wonder why a God-loving single man or woman did not become a priest or nun. Did it never occur to them that one might like living the single life as such and not want to be a member of a clerical or vowed community? That one could serve God beautifully in the single vocation, enjoy gifts of friendship and love other people?

In the face of these and like assumptions, single persons often found it best to remain silent, lest they appear overly defensive of their vocation. Still, it hurt to be the victim of such stereotypes.

In more recent times, singles seemed to go to the opposite extreme—from being bound by role models to trying to live a limit-free existence. It was as if freedom meant doing whatever one felt like doing. In the name of being mature, many resorted to an adolescent approach to life. If life was without limits, options could be picked up and discarded like daffodils. Morality was only a repressive burden; religion was an illusion; all that mattered was self-actualization.

Little wonder this era gave birth to the "swinging single." To be single burgeoned in popularity. There were all kinds of ways to live alone and like it. Above all, singleness was equated with the myth of total freedom. Many prided themselves on not being entrapped by permanent commitments. Stay-for-a-while-and-then-move-on became more the rule than the exception.

The single style of life was held up as the model of a well-managed existence. One could schedule activities or stay at home; seek action or learn through the help of techniques and seminars how to deal with apathy; be in control of one's space and time. Many singles became models of self-assertion, self-sufficiency and self-gratification. They were satisfied, actualized and, of course, self-affirmed. They would decide who would or who would not invade their space and for how long. Mobility was upward. Careers came first, and neither family nor colleagues nor friends could stand in the way.

Worst of all, singleness became a defense against marriage, making it the lesser state, just as singleness used to be lesser when compared to marriage. People bought the popular idea that they could have the best of both worlds: live like singles and on the side, be married; live for one's career and on the side, take care or have others take care of the children; live like a secular man or woman in the world and still be a priest or sister. If before the role models were rigid, now they were practically nonexistent. Strange that with so many people making it, so few seemed happy.

Even as I write this book, it seems clear that ego-frustration has set in. The swinging era is at least beginning to question itself. Having tried everything, having made every conceivable human and technical effort to be happy, people still experience a vast hollowness within, a pervasive wasteland void of meaning. Is there something we have missed? Is there anything more we can turn to? Is the search for fulfillment moving toward spiritual horizons, and, if so, what are the implications for single living?

RESPONDING TO OUR SPIRITUAL HUNGER

The experience of ego-frustration offers fertile ground in which a foundational spiritual formation can flourish. A friend of mine put it this way: "When you get up in the morning and can no longer bear the sight of yourself in the mirror, you look beyond and through the glass darkly to God." This renewed foundational experience of faith preserves the childlike trust that enables us to bind ourselves to that which is more than we are. It encourages us not to repress our spiritual hunger but to cry out of the depths for God's help.

We have in part to thank the feats of the technological era for promoting this spiritual awakening. Through the communications media, we can attain a global consciousness that lessens narcissism. We are aware of the need to foster a just distribution of the world's goods while adventuring toward new frontiers of scientific discovery. Breakthroughs in medicine and physics have made us more conscious of the mysterious intertwining of micro- and macrocosm. Time once again is invaded by timeless mysteries. Human structures seem to be sustained by a vast and divinely ordered superstructure.

True, this era also produced "masters of suspicion" like Freud, Marx and Nietzsche, who exploded our assumptions about God. If God was really a projection of human needs, then religion was an opium of the people. It had to be destroyed by the enlightened minds of atheists, but surely atheism or agnosticism cannot be the only alternatives to eroded religion. The spirit may be dampened, but the flame of faith does not die that easily. There is in the human spirit an insatiable desire for God. From the fragments of disillusion and near despair, there can emerge a new era of belief. Such is what we witness today.

As history testifies, aberrations and extremes accompany the start of any new age. Spirituality is not excluded from this tendency. The ancient temptation to be all-body or all-spirit raises its head. We could say that the material side of this temptation strives to invest the entire transcendent in a person or group or code of conduct. Such an attempt often gives rise to the cult phenomenon that attracts many young people. Religion in this case becomes a mode of magic or manipulation, providing the naïve disciple with all the answers and precluding personal reflection. Disciples may be in even deeper trouble when the cult is headed by a charismatic figure, whose mannerisms can mesmerize the feelings and conscience of a person. The quintessential example in our time is Jonestown.

On the spiritualistic side of the temptation to extremism, one may equate religion with exotic phenomena that promise escape from ordinary reality into cosmic being. Common examples find people making a religion out of palm reading or horoscopic predictions. Certain kinds of Eastern meditation techniques may lead the advocate to an out-of-this-world experience that rejects organized religion and seeks ever more spectacular "spiritual highs" via chanting, fasting, eating special foods or whatever. Some "religious" experiences are even induced by chemical means. The body is a tool through which one gets beyond earthly existence.

Singles interested in a spiritual life necessarily come in contact with these extremist options, but they resist being labeled spinsters or swingers, cultists or spiritualists. They want to see their life either temporarily or permanently as a response made in reflective solitude to One greater than they are. They want to be a healthy, wholesome, unique expression of the God in whose image and likeness they have been formed. They want to explore fully their gifts of creativity; to feel deeply the whole mystery of being embodied spirits; to live in dedication to the betterment of the world. They know that the longing they experience for something more can only be quieted in union with the transcendent.

To be a single person of spiritual depth may mean in our time to witness by one's life for the tension between apparently irreconcilable yet ultimately united formation powers. I mean feeling and reason; incarnation and inspiration; action and contemplation; dedication and detachment; singularity and universality; worldliness and transworldly wisdom; being one and being together. The list could go on but, suffice it to say, the challenge of singleness is to move away from an *either-or* posture toward living in the *both-and* mystery of life.

Singleness is a way of life that sets one on the line between the known and the unknowable, between certitude and insecurity, between assurance and surrender. To be single, one has to be willing to meet life courageously, delighting in its advances and reversals, its resonance and resistance, while growing increasingly aware of a higher power toward whom one is in the end only a servant.

Single life is made up of this tension, this coincidence of opposites, this coinherence of limits and possibilities. One must be alert yet subdued, eager to lead yet willing to follow, worthwhile in oneself yet only too aware of the need for humility. Happily, for the single person who is Christian, the model for this way is Christ. Loneliness is more and more interpreted as a call from the Lord. This state of being alone is but a reminder of that insatiable yearning to be with others and God that is at the heart of all human experience.

RESPONDING TO OUR CALL TO SINGLENESS

It follows that a vocation to the single life, like any other calling, must be compatible with one's temperament and talents, with one's personal and social gifts and limits. We must feel that this calling is congenial with who we truly are. Some people are single, but they are not really happy in this state; they would prefer to be married if the right person came along. Others find living alone impossibly demanding and would welcome the support offered by an established community.

We must acknowledge, by the same token, that there may be some people who married early in life without sufficient vocational appraisal, or who joined religious communities in late adolescence and now wish they had remained single in the world. Be this as it may, we make our choices at key times in life and we have to live with them.

Today one finds a number of persons who have thoughtfully committed themselves, perhaps in their late twenties or thirties, to the single vocation as such. These persons have always lived alone in the world in adulthood, meaning that they have never been married nor have they been members of a conventual or diocesan establishment. Many others find themselves single, for example, due to separation, divorce, death of a spouse, or dispensation from the priesthood or some form of vowed religious life.

Among this latter group many may also be awaiting the right spouse or desirous of rejoining some established community. Still others may be on the verge of making a commitment to the single vocation and need some help in exploring the rich possibilities of living alone in the world, with or without secondary attachment to some support association composed of friends or colleagues who share similar ideals.

I hope that any single person reading this book who may

have doubted his or her vocation will feel reconfirmed in this choice, recognizing anew its human and Christian potential and encouraging others who may have a similar calling to follow it.

Suggested Readings

Bronowski, Jacob. *The Ascent of Man.* Boston: Little, Brown & Company, 1973.

Bronowski's panoramic overview of the intellectual history of civilization brims over with the author's fascination with humans and the laudable qualities which give them a unique place in the cosmos: dexterity, observation, thoughtfulness and passion. The author demonstrates that the most powerful drive in the ascent of man is his pleasure in his own skill, his innate desire and need to function effectively in giving form to his life and world. Human persons are unique because they are able, through marvelous plasticity of mind, to be both scientists and artists in their world.

Eliot, T. S. *The Complete Poems and Plays, 1909–1950.* New York: Harcourt, Brace & Company, Inc., 1952.

An inspiring collection of poems and plays for those who seek an intuitive appreciation of the role of the individual and the community in modern technological society. The poems include "Prufrock," "The Waste Land," "The Hollow Men," "Ash Wednesday," "Choruses from 'The Rock'" and "Four Quartets." The plays include *Murder in the Cathedral, The Family Reunion* and *The Cocktail Party.*

Ellul, Jacques. *The Technological Society.* Trans. John Wilkinson. New York: Alfred A. Knopf, 1967.

Ellul's examination of our progressively technical civilization demonstrates that the ever-expanding and irreversible rule of technique is extended to all domains of life. Persons in a pervasively technological society may be deformed by a tendency to view ends as means and to prize a thing only for its ability to help achieve something else. Ellul's book inspires profound reconsideration of personal values: emotional, intellectual and spiritual.

Lasch, Christopher. *The Culture of Narcissism*. New York: W. W. Norton, 1978.

An analysis of the "narcissistic personality of our time," this book identifies some of the major obstacles to spirituality and originality in American society today. Out of fear of being labeled a loser, the narcissist labels himself a "winner," that is, he or she identifies with the admired and envied image of the outer-directed successful person. The emptiness and isolation of modern bureaucracies favor narcissism rather than the cultivation of uniqueness and originality.

Needleman, Jacob. *The New Religions*. New York: Doubleday, 1970.

In this text, the author reviews developments in the "new religions" prevalent in the United States since the 1960s—such as Zen Buddhism; the teachings of Meher Baba; transcendental meditation; Gurdjieff's explanations of a new way of living; and religious interest in astrology, reincarnation, drugs and other forms of popular enthusiasm.

Ricoeur, Paul. "Religion, Atheism, and Faith." *The Religious Significance of Atheism*. New York: Columbia University Press, 1966.

In this philosophical evaluation of the religious significance of atheism, Ricoeur sees atheism not necessarily as a negation and destruction of religion but as a potential to clear the ground for a new faith for a post-religious age. Atheism stands between religion and faith as both a break and a link. In its twofold role as destroyer of the shelter offered by religion and liberator from the taboos imposed by religion, atheism clears the ground for a mature faith which overcomes archaic systems.

Tournier, Paul. *The Whole Person in a Broken World*. Trans. John Doberstein and Helen Doberstein. New York: Harper & Row, Publishers, 1964.

In this book, the author compares the spiritual crisis of today's world with the defiance of adolescent youth, revolting against the tutorship of the past, yet unable to find the freedom and independence of spiritual maturity. In pointing the way to methods of treatment, his direct, compelling biblical faith cuts across all denominational lines and speaks to that lonely place where we know that only reconciliation with God in Christ can make us wholly true and truly whole. Tournier deals with such topics as the inner conflict of modern man, the rift between the spiritual and the temporal, the myth of progress and power and the task of the Church.

van Kaam, Adrian. *Personality Fulfillment in the Spiritual Life.* Denville, N.J.: Dimension Books, 1966.
This is an inspiring reflection on religious presence and the life of the spirit. As incarnated spirit, the person is truly involved in everyday endeavors while at the same time transcending them. The life of the spirit inspires an attitude of reverence and respect for the sacredness of persons, things and events. Refusal of the sacred dimension leads to a violent attitude and to escape in counterfeit modes of presence. The "threefold path" of obedience, chastity and poverty of spirit is presented for persons in all forms of life: single, married, priestly and conventual.

——. *The Transcendent Self.* Denville, N.J.: Dimension Books, 1979.
While focusing on the phenomenon of the midlife crisis, this text reflects on the challenge and opportunity inherent in all crises to deepen our insight into the basic dynamics of human formation. Detailed attention is given to the actual nature of self-transcendence, both its positive and negative stages, to aid one's own gradual spiritual unfolding from lower to higher forms of life.

——. "Provisional Glossary of the Terminology of the Science of Foundational Formative Spirituality." *Studies in Formative Spirituality,* I, 1 (February 1980), pp. 137–56.
The first publication of terminology for the new Science of Foundational Formation being developed at the Institute of Formative Spirituality, these glossary terms elaborate on the concept of formation as a fundamental guiding insight into the capacity for growth and transformation of all creation. This issue focuses specifically on the dynamic powers, sources, forms and dimensions characteristic of human formation.

2

✳✳✳✳✳✳✳✳✳✳✳✳✳✳✳✳✳✳
✳✳✳✳✳✳✳✳✳✳✳✳✳✳✳✳✳

In Celebration
of Singleness

Being alone is a neutral condition, conducive to formation in the single life, depending on how we respond to it. Due to circumstances and inner attitudes, we may experience this state in one of two ways: as *a-loneness* (the pain of being lonely) or as *all-oneness* (the joy of solitude). We must not conclude that a spiritual life rescues single persons from the pain of loneliness. It does not. Many times I've been acutely aware of my singleness and really felt lonely: preparing a meal for one, asking for a single table in a restaurant, feeling out of it in the midst of a laughing crowd. Sometimes I wake up at night and wonder what will happen to me when I grow old and sick and no spouse or children, no fellow community members, are there to take care of me.

This awareness of my aloneness could cause me to become anxious and depressed were I to dwell excessively on it. Instead I try to remember the positive, spiritual meaning and the psychological contentment that comes with being single: blessing my quiet apartment at the end of a busy day, staying in or going out as I please, calling a friend or silencing the ring on my phone so I can spend the evening reading and praying. Loneliness slowly changes into solitude also when I recommit myself to the Lord and enjoy His companionship.

This remembrance of Another can mark the transition point between the pain of loneliness and the joy of solitude. I realize that no human companion, no matter how wonderful, can quell our innate longing for oneness with God. Behind all faces, His is the face each of us seeks lastingly to behold.

In solitude I bring my whole being—physical, emotional, spiritual—before God and ask Him for the grace I need to live my single calling joyfully. I do not want to fall into self-pity or madly seek some meaningful encounter. God knows I need His help to live a harmonious inner and outer life, avoiding the either/or extremes that often tempt singles: either too much withdrawal or too much involvement.

Personally, as a Christian, I try to center my singleness in the heart of Jesus, the Single Word spoken by the Father. In the Word made flesh, I am at home with my single calling and united spiritually with all other people, contemplatively present to His will and actively serving the members of His kingdom.

In this light, being alone takes on a new meaning. Far from being a negative experience of isolation and withdrawal, singleness as solitude is the root of solidarity and communion. Oneness in God is the ground out of which togetherness emerges. Sharing is possible because we belong uniquely to the same Divine Parent. If, with God's help, we can make this shift from a-loneness to all-oneness, we can enjoy the rich benefits of the single life as an avenue to realistic self-awareness and creative participation in the culture.

SOLITUDE FORMS US SPIRITUALLY AND SOCIALLY

Let us look further into the formative meaning of solitude in the life of a single person. Every human experiences both distance from others based on our uniqueness, and nearness to others because of our alikeness. Single persons are quite conscious of this dynamic tension. One feels the contrast between human greatness in relation to the microcosm, and human wretchedness and nothingness in the face of cosmic majesty.

Two apparently contradictory statements of Blaise Pascal capture the essential tension of fearing yet befriending aloneness.[1] He wrote in his *Pensées*, "The eternal silence of these infinite spaces fills me with dread." But a complement to that fearful remark in the same text posits: "The sole cause of man's unhappiness is that he does not know how to stay quietly in his room." In that room there is terror, but there is also terrible beauty.

To be single is to live in the tension between loneliness and solitude, recollection and communion, detachment and encounter. Once I agreed to serve as co-host for a group of graduate students who were participating in a course on faith formation. We booked accommodations at a nearby retreat center from Friday evening to Sunday afternoon. For several hours after supper on Friday and all day on Saturday, we met for conferences followed by small group sessions. By Saturday evening I felt a physical, if not a spiritual, need to get away from the students and other teachers to regain perspective on what we were sharing. I knew that if I didn't seek some solitude, I might get lost in surface issues and lose my sense of deeper meanings. It also happens at times that aloneness becomes too much to endure and I need to be with good companions. I remember feeling rather low one evening after a demanding round of meetings with university administrators. To lock my door and be home alone was more than I could bear. I phoned a friend, shared my plight and found her more than willing to drop everything and go with me to dinner and a movie. We saw a good comedy and spent the rest of the evening talking and laughing.

Being single enables me to take distance from the pressures of family and community living, while at the same time

---

[1] Blaise Pascal, *Pensées*, as quoted in Hans Küng, *Does God Exist?* (New York: Doubleday, 1978), pp. 52, 54.

it offers a chance for welcome contact at festivities, weekend visits and holiday seasons. In some ways one does live in the best of both worlds, thus accounting for one of the major attractions of this vocation. But any life-style, while opening up possibilities, also has its limits—and singleness is no exception.

One does experience the need for distance, and this in turn can lead to frequent bouts with loneliness. The deepest why of this distance has to do with one's desire to assess situations from a transcendent perspective rather than being trapped in sheer trivia. Any thoughtful person can feel this way, but in singles it is likely to become a passion. I myself feel unhappy if I'm outside the quiet of my room for long periods of time. Each of us has a limit to socializing. At times I have to simply say good-bye to friends and family to be alone for a while.

Such distancing is not an occasion for self-indulgence or an escape from involvement but an honest response to a unique feature of the single life call. This reflective bent in no way makes single persons smarter or holier than their married or religious counterparts, for holiness is a matter of grace and goodwill. Distancing for the sake of reflection is simply one indelible mark of the single life assumed as a serious vocation. Stepping aside is no sacrifice; it is more like second nature. I need to be with people, but I also need to be away from them. Even married couples crave that alone time once in a while.

Understood spiritually, solitude grants single persons the distance and time they need to assess God's will as manifested in the life situation. Short-run solutions to a problem may be expedient, but their effects are ephemeral. Usually these facile answers ignore or evade totally the perspective of transcendence. It is precisely this long-range view that interests single persons.

As an aside, one can see what an asset a committed single person is to his or her profession. Thoughtful approaches to complex matters are among their strongest points because they are freed from immediate familial and communal demands and distractions.

The Faith Commitment of
Single Persons to the Hidden Life

Living in singleness not only makes one more perceptive of the will of God in events and people. It can also increase the courage to stand up for values in which we believe and to resist being swept along by the tide of popular opinion. A faithful single person may be called at times to be a sign of contradiction, as Jesus was. Anyone who witnesses to perennial human and Christian values is bound to be at odds on some points with the commercial or political stands of contemporary societies anywhere in the world.

For instance, Christian moral and spiritual values will always pose painful questions to a society that mocks permanent commitment and recommends that we all do our own thing. This attitude must be contradicted by adherents of a religion that holds to certain revealed, objective truths.

As a guardian of these values, the single person, strengthened by the grace of solitude, is better able to resist the push and pull of the present age. In my singleness, I believe that the worst crime I could commit is to forfeit my freedom to the compulsions of a crowd that finds safety in big numbers and impressive statistics. What could be worse than to relinquish the gift of spiritual formation into the hands of a leveling collectivity that reduces human need merely to its physical or functional dimensions, neglecting wholly the thirst for transcendence?

The same faith commitment that motivates a person's choice of singleness sustains his or her devotion to foundational human values. These are usually lived in a hidden way, but at times one may be compelled by grace and nature to go public. Because singles are accustomed to aloneness from early in life, they know what it feels like to stand on their own two feet and to treasure the freedom from crowd compulsions this commitment brings.

When we cease to find peace within ourselves, when we lose our allegiance to God, we risk becoming enslaved to utilitarian values. As interest in higher human potentials wanes, we may find ourselves becoming fixated on certain fads. We forget what it feels like to be our own self, responsible for our eternal soul. We buy into the myth that our species is collective and that our worth consists in serving the colony, as ants or wasps do. Life is reduced to an endless round of eating, working, spending and sleeping. One ceases to take pride in one's task and does as little as possible to get a paycheck. Lacking a foundational, reflective stance, life drones away from birth to death, its deeper meaning hidden from view, its seed of divinity stunted or snuffed out.[2]

The specter of such a repression of human dignity stimulates us as single persons, who celebrate uniqueness, to stand up for our beliefs, even if we have to suffer loneliness and unpopularity. The pain is well worth it. To suffer for the sake of human rights and freedoms is a blessing. It binds my heart to the suffering heart of Christ. Ridicule did not prevent Him from remaining faithful to spiritual truths, and neither must it deter His followers.

Not surprisingly, we often find single persons in the forefront of spiritual leadership. They have a keen sense of the kingdom of God already operative in this world. They welcome the suffering that enables them to reflect more realistically on Christ-centered directives and to live these out in decision and action. The singleness of such Christians as Søren Kierkegaard, Dag Hammarskjöld and Flannery O'Connor made them available for an apostolate of creativity —in philosophizing, in the political arena, in artistic and social commentary. Their lives remind us that one of the privileges of singleness is that we enjoy more time to devote to the

[2] See Arianna Stassinopoulos, *After Reason* (New York: Stein and Day, 1978), pp. 98–99.

pursuit of creativity and community service, since less time has to be spent in family activities. This freedom carries with it certain responsibilities, of which leadership and the preservation of spiritual values are but two.

A spirituality of the single life never makes singleness an end in itself, but sees it as a graced opportunity to orient one's life toward some kind of self-giving activity related to one's profession and position. This service may be public, but more often than not it is hidden. Active, dynamic single people usually lead a hidden life in the spiritual sense. While often being gifted, outgoing communicators, they need to retire in stillness. The imprint of their uniqueness appears in whatever they are doing, from preparing a meal to addressing an audience, but many are shy about calling attention to themselves. The figures mentioned (Kierkegaard, Hammarskjöld, O'Connor) are excellent examples. Only in their diaries and letters do we learn of their being "spies for the Eternal," who conducted secret negotiations between God and man.[3] They must have known that the fruits of their actions would speak louder than boastful words.

As Adrian van Kaam insightfully remarks in his book *On Being Yourself*, the original person does not need to invent new forms of life or display unusual talents. He or she may simply do what many others do in the environment. Their originality shines through not in what they do but in the way they do it, not in the customs they have but in the way they live them.[4] In his same text, applying his thinking to the Christian called to die to the old self, van Kaam writes that this directive does not mean that Christians lose their identity or fuse with the Godhead. It means that as a Christian I

[3] See Søren Kierkegaard, *The Point of View for My Work as an Author: A Report to History*, trans. Walter Lowrie (New York: Harper & Row, Publishers, Harper Torchbooks, 1962); Dag Hammarskjöld, *Markings*, trans. Leif Sjöberg and W. H. Auden (New York: Alfred A. Knopf, 1969); and Flannery O'Connor, *The Habit of Being: Letters of Flannery O'Connor*, ed. Sally Fitzgerald (New York: Farrar, Straus, & Giroux, 1979).

[4] Adrian van Kaam, *On Being Yourself: Reflections on Spirituality and Originality* (Denville, N.J.: Dimension Books, 1972), pp. 21–22.

should distance myself from false self-images. In van Kaam's words:

> *I should not strive after an isolated God-like self. I must give up self-centered plans and projects. I must find my original self hidden in God. The original life of a Christian, as St. Paul says, is hidden in Christ. The Eternal Father originates each one of us in Him.*[5]

True spiritual formation is best understood in light of this hidden spiritual potential, this self-transcending tendency. It is this thrust toward transcendence that distinguishes human persons from all other creatures, for within our human spirit resides the Spirit of God. His Spirit draws us to silent adoration while at the same time inviting us to proclaim to the world by our being alone the good news of oneness with Him.

Referring again to van Kaam's *On Being Yourself,* we read that each person is called to become his or her own self and yet to become at-one with God. He writes:

> *I must become the unique person I am meant to be. The more I become what my Creator called me to be originally, the more I will be united with my Divine Origin. This union with my Origin deepens my originality. Mine is an originality that God wills from eternity. He originated me as precisely this person and nobody else.*[6]

In this description we sense anew the healthy tension between being alone and being at-one.

To grow ever more like the One we love, in whose image and likeness we are created, is the goal of the hidden life. Any promise of utopia on earth is a meaningless illusion com-

[5] Ibid., pp. 7–8.
[6] Ibid., p. 8.

pared to this gift of union. We can only be whole, and therefore most single, when we are hidden in the Holy, our original Source. "In these depths," says van Kaam, "I feel at-one
with God. I feel also at-one with every person and thing that
merges from this same Divine Ground."[7] In the words of St.
Paul: "I live now not with my own life but with the life of
Christ who lives in me." (Ga. 2:20)

The heart of the single person must thus become more
and more like the heart of Jesus, who listened to the voice of
the Father and to the voice of people who sought His care.
Our first concern must be to respond to His call in the depths
of our being. We know from experience how tempting it is to
close our ears to the hidden voice of the Lord when the
voices of the multitude clamor for attention. We must recall
at such moments the conflict Christ Himself felt as a single
person. He wanted to respond to the needs of the crowds who
followed Him, but first He chose to retire in solitude to listen
to the voice of the Father. He stepped aside to mountaintops
and desert places to ready Himself for a demanding mission.
For about thirty years His uniquely original and spiritual life
was formed with His parents in the village of Nazareth. On
the foundation of these private years He would go forth for a
few public years to reveal the meaning and value of living
one's whole life as an act of self-donating love for God and
neighbor.

Like the Lord, we too must become a forming, healing
presence in the world, witnessing to the joyful spirituality of a
single life that progresses through solitude to an increasing
depth of intimacy with the Lord and ministry to other people.
In our singleheartedness we must try to discover a meaning
that transcends gratification of immediate needs and points
toward the lasting fulfillment that can only be ours in eternity.

If this potential for Spirit-inspired action lies dormant,
what is best in us dies. Worse still, if our longing for transcen-

[7] Ibid., p. 25.

dence is displaced by ego-centered motives—like politics of power, idolatry of affluence, hedonistic pleasure—we are doomed to disappointment. The only absolute is God. As St. Augustine said after years of searching elsewhere for the answers: "For Thou hast made us for Thyself and our hearts are restless till they rest in Thee."[8]

In Thee means just that. No other person or thing, situation or event, can ultimately offer us the wholeness and harmony we seek. Single persons resonate with St. Teresa of Avila's advice to her sisters when she told them emphatically: "God alone suffices." We long in the end to hide ourselves in Him, to rest in the shelter of His wings (Ps. 61). This experience of a hidden and profound joy led me to write in my journal this brief but heartfelt prayer:

Lord,
it is enough
that you alone
see and know
who I am and
what I am doing.

It is enough
that you are aware
of what my life as
a single person
is all about.

Witnessing as Singles to a Joyful Spirituality

Though in the end I know we must all die alone, I also believe that God is calling us beyond loneliness to a new life of oneness. As a single woman, I want to witness to a way of living that liberates me from inordinate attachment to the

[8] *The Confessions of Saint Augustine*, Books I–X, trans. F. J. Sheed (Kansas City: Sheed, Andrews and McMeel, 1970), p. 3.

world of power, pleasure and possession so that I can serve the Lord as an instrument of transformation. My singleness frees me to see God's image in creation so that I can reverence the earth as His dwelling place, as the House of God. Living from this faith horizon, I am free to flow with God's will in the situation, free to travel lightly, unencumbered by the weight of self-will and its futile projects of salvation.

Paradoxically, the highest moment of human uniqueness is ours when we lose ourselves in Him. This loss gives way to the liberation of the selves we truly are, loved by God and free to give His love to others.

Living in peaceful presence to the Divine Origin of self, others and world, I am neither overwhelmed by personal failure nor overly proud of my success. I try to do the best I can in times of suffering and temptation, always aware in tranquil gratitude of the changeless love of the Lord. He strengthens me to endure the conflicts and challenges of these changing times without betraying the integrity of my single vocation.

Singleness is thus destined to generate a joyful spirituality that enables us to serve God in whatever walk of life He places us. The single soul is able to soar free and to experience moments of playful carelessness because of its being cared for by God. Such graced experiences transform us into grateful people who live in happy dependence upon the merciful kindness of our loving Lord. Our whole life is an exercise in gratitude as we try to reproduce His goodness in our own attitudes and actions.

How sad that many associate singleness with long, gloomy faces and endless frustrations. The limits of this life open up exciting possibilities for meaning and creativity. The vocation to the single life offers an opportunity for solitude and communion, for reflection and action, for an awareness of and a witness to the oneness each of us experiences in the heart of Christ.

Single persons are thus conscious of living here and now on the road to eternity. On this road we go out of ourselves in love for others because we are all loved by the Other. By sharing our joys and pains, our hopes and disappointments, our realities and dreams, our affections and detachments, we tell our companions on the road that they are not really alone, that a loving, caring God is with them always. To love in this way calls for a depth of emotional and spiritual maturity and, above all, a consuming vision of the world as the House of God, and all of us as His children, called singly by name.

Suggested Readings

Augustine. *The Confessions of Saint Augustine.* Trans. John K. Ryan. Garden City, N.Y.: Doubleday, Image Books, 1960.

This classic is a personal account of the search for truth and eventual conversion by one of the outstanding figures of Western Christianity. It is a confession of the author's sin and error in the face of God's goodness and truth as well as a confident proclamation of the divine rest that awaits us at the end of our spiritual journey.

Boros, Ladislaus. *Pain and Providence.* Trans. Edward Quinn. New York: The Seabury Press, 1975.

This is a book for those who want to be the authors of their own lives, to put some sense into them, to see some pattern in their existence—a most difficult task when pain and suffering, frustration and cruelty seem to dominate one's life and the world at large. How to reconcile pain with providence, how to see providence working through pain, is the lesson of a lifetime, the secret of Christian wisdom and the gift of this text.

Hammarskjöld, Dag. *Markings.* Trans. Leif Sjöberg and W. H. Auden. New York: Alfred A. Knopf, 1969.

The diary of an intensely dedicated public servant, *Markings* profiles Hammarskjöld's gradual discovery of what it means to say "yes" to one's neighbor and one's fate, first as a civil servant in his homeland, Sweden, and then as Secretary-General to the United Nations. Hammarskjöld remained single throughout his life and saw himself as a man with a mission, as a servant of peace in a hostile and overly political world. The diary, a modern spiritual document, chronicles the strength one man derived from his sense of communion with God.

Kierkegaard, Søren. *The Point of View for My Work as an Author: A Report to History*. Trans. Walter Lowrie. New York: Harper & Row, Publishers, Harper Torchbooks, 1962.

The category of "the individual," as put forth in this work, assumes a missionary role for the Christian *within* Christendom. The single individual stands alone before God, in obedience, and serves his neighbor by making persons (i.e., Christians) into Christians. Humanity needs eternity and it is only a return to the formative tradition of Christianity that can carry a person to what is essential, true and eternal.

——. *The Present Age*. Trans. Alexander Dru. New York: Harper & Row, Publishers, Harper Torchbooks, 1962.

In *The Present Age* Kierkegaard once again takes up the question of how one should live. He is especially critical of the fact that more and more people renounce the quiet and modest tasks of life that are so important and pleasing to God, in order to achieve something greater. *The Present Age* laments the loss of authority, especially the loss of a deeply Christian formation tradition which Christ founded and which the individual needs to be grounded securely in the world.

Merton, Thomas. *Contemplation in a World of Action*. New York: Doubleday, Image Books, 1973.

In this text, Merton calls for the renewal of "the primitive simplicity and authenticity of the monastic life" and for a certain distance from society that permits fruitful "contemplation in a world of action." These essays represent his clearest statements about the monastic life. His case for the eremitical vocation is not based on hatred for humanity but simply on the premise that "some of us *have to be* alone to be ourselves." The reflections on renewal are particularly relevant in our time when so many persons are seeking new and personally meaningful forms of human and Christian living.

O'Connor, Flannery. *The Habit of Being: Letters of Flannery O'Connor*. Ed. Sally Fitzgerald. New York: Farrar, Straus, & Giroux, 1979.

This collection of letters, written by the American novelist and short-story writer, is a simple yet profoundly human testimony to the underlying meaning of the author's life and work. With a sometimes humorous, sometimes intense, but always penetrating style, Flannery restores lived dignity and value to both the pain and the promise of single life.

Pascal, Blaise. *Pensées*. Trans. W. F. Trotter. New York: E. P. Dutton & Co., A Dutton Paperback, 1958.

These notes for a projected defense of Christianity are a compelling example of the need for recovery of a spiritual dimension in human life. In his "thoughts," Pascal recommends living in the mystery of a higher calling if we want to seek and experience the satisfaction and peace of the whole person.

Stassinopoulos, Arianna. *After Reason*. New York: Stein and Day, 1978.

This is an articulate treatment of modern arrogance with its materialist passion and delusion that human society can recreate itself through politics. The author suggests that our first task is to rescue the human imagination from the rationalist rubble of our time. The failure of the Social Revolution, the Sexual Revolution and the Drug Revolution to fulfill their promises is one among many growing signs that the crucial battle in our age is that of the individual for the meaning of his or her own life. According to the author, this spiritual awakening is a yearning unparalleled in history.

van Kaam, Adrian; van Croonenburg, Bert; and Muto, Susan. *The Emergent Self*. Denville, N.J.: Dimension Books, 1968.

A collection of short, inspiring meditations on life and living in the light of the human experience of the self; the self and others; the self and community; and the self and world. We are called to live in a balanced, ultimately transformed, rhythm of receptivity and response to the mystery of our unique spiritual formation.

——; van Croonenburg, Bert; and Muto, Susan. *The Participant Self*. Denville, N.J.: Dimension Books, 1969.

A sequel to *The Emergent Self*, this text explores the cycle of participation and recollection necessary for living a spiritual life. Interpersonal involvement and opportunities to dwell in recollected presence to the meaning of communal experiences are complementary phases, both illuminating and nourishing the gradual unfolding of God's plan in our lives.

van Kaam, Adrian. *On Being Involved: The Rhythm of Involvement and Detachment in Daily Life*. Denville, N.J.: Dimension Books, 1970.

Beyond our inner divisions and distractions, there is a basic rhythm of involvement and detachment in the spiritual life. Through the recurring phases of death, decision and rebirth, we are led gradually from a dominant inclination to self-centeredness to a peaceful, unified encounter with the sacred dimension of reality.

——. *On Being Yourself: Reflections on Spirituality and Originality.* Denville, N.J.: Dimension Books, 1972.

Based on the principle that to be truly human means to choose one's true self, this text describes the overall process of and obstacles to original personality growth. To discover our true selves requires that we relate in an authentic way to the world and to others. Then, day by day with God's grace, we may rise to the fullness of Christian presence.

——. *The Dynamics of Spiritual Self-Direction.* Denville, N.J.: Dimension Books, 1976.

The author describes in detail our capacity for discovering our unique, spiritual self-direction in God. Over a lifetime process of successive self-alienation and emergence, we learn to restructure our lives according to the unique direction God gives to every person, gradually incarnating our transcendent destiny in everyday life.

——. "Provisional Glossary of the Terminology of the Science of Foundational Formation." *Studies in Formative Spirituality*, I, 2 (May 1980), pp. 287–304.

Expanding the theory of human and Christian formation, this glossary reflects on the scope of the formation perspective and its interrelationship with other theories of human development. Further entries consider the dynamic characteristics of foundational formation; the sources of formation; and the horizons of specific formation acts and forms.

3

✲✲✲✲✲✲✲✲✲✲✲✲✲✲✲✲✲✲✲
✲✲✲✲✲✲✲✲✲✲✲✲✲✲✲✲✲✲

Single by Circumstance—
A Spiritual Perspective

Many reading this "celebration of singleness" may not feel like celebrating at all. If anything, they may feel more frustrated than ever because they did not choose to be single. They find themselves single because of circumstances outside their control or preference.

While I cannot help anyone concretely to find a way out of this circumstance, I may be able to offer some thoughts pertaining to ways of living within it from a spiritual or formative perspective. What happens when one's singleness is neither fully appraised nor freely chosen? This question may rightly be asked by readers who are separated or divorced, widowed at a fairly young age, or elderly, or unmarried for whatever reason. The circumstances may be different, but the outcome is the same. One is single without entirely wanting to be this way. Rather than focusing on how to change this circumstance, the question before us is: How can we make sense of it spiritually?

It must be a terrible feeling to wake up alone in a bed that until recently was occupied by a spouse. A friend of my mother's told me that after her husband died she could not slip over onto his side of the bed for the longest time.

A relative separated from his wife after twenty years of

marriage called to say that he feels miserable dining alone but despises even more the indignity of being thought "fair game." I encouraged him in his pursuit of solitude while seeking to widen his circle of understanding friends.

A colleague of mine, who is thirty-three years old, could not believe that she actually returned her engagement ring. She asked me to help her face the loneliness of the first dateless Saturday night in months. Yet she knew in her heart that this man was not the right person for her. She could not marry him, but would there ever be another eligible man in her life?

One could go on listing case after case of people who find themselves alone and who are really not convinced that the single life is for them. Yet they may not want to marry or seek another binding form of community. They feel as if they are between railroad stations and not sure where this ticket to life will lead them. A number of people may be bitter about the destiny they've been given, but the vast majority want to discover some meaning in this initially stark realization that they are single for one reason or another.

What does one do in this time of transition? For some it may pass, but for just as many it may be a permanent state. One's age may be a major factor in deciding whether the single state is only a time of transition to marriage or another kind of communal commitment. People who are single in the age range of eighteen to thirty-five may rightly regard this as a temporal phase on the way to a more permanent commitment.

When one remains single or finds oneself single after that, it is wise to at least raise the question of whether or not God is calling one to live the single life itself as a permanent vocation. When one is younger, life does seem to hold many more possibilities. One's basic attitude may be that of carefree exploration. After age thirty-five, people may begin to face the fact of their personal and social limits. This awareness may be depressing at first, but in the end it may prove an opportune moment for spiritual deepening.

A forty-two-year-old colleague of mine shared her experience of being separated from her husband after eighteen years of marriage. For a while she admitted to being plagued by doubt and self-pity. She sought some needed counseling to help her recover from the shock of being single. In a stark way she had to confront the breakup of her marriage and the responsibility of custody for three teenage children. After the transition period and several months of supportive counseling, she was able to regain her composure, becoming, in her words, "a strong lady."

What was the source of her newly recovered strength? Luckily for her, she had always been a person whose faith in God was not easily shaken. She attributed this conviction to her initial formation at home. Though she felt angry at God for a while and went through bouts of depression, she felt underneath these painful circumstances a source of strength that had to come from God. Nothing else could explain the conviction that she had not been abandoned entirely. She wanted to find a transcendent meaning in all that had happened to her.

In this woman's experience I believe there is a message for those who find themselves single. It may be difficult, if not impossible, to make sense of this situation unless one is willing to explore these events from a faith perspective. Is this circumstance just one mosaic in a transitional pattern, or the portend of a permanent calling to the single life?

WHAT IS GOD TRYING TO TELL ME?

By tracing briefly some typical stages of spiritual deepening one may find an answer. An event like finding oneself single after years of marriage marks the transition from one current form of life to another. At the onset this transition is characterized by conflict. Things that were once taken for granted are now brought into question. One feels suddenly vulnerable. The harmony is broken. Yet in this breaking up of old patterns of life new directives break through. When life as one knows it falls apart, one can ask the faith question: "What is God trying to tell me?"

With this question, one moves from complacency about one's life direction to a more serious reflection on it. If this event is utterly meaningless, then life itself is only a hit-or-miss proposition. One may be tempted to shun God and never trust Him. A more creative response is to open one's heart to Him in this suffering and seek an answer through reflection and prayer. In due time one may gain some sense of reintegration, some capacity to forgive those who hurt or betrayed one and to grow in compassion. Let me recall another experience to illustrate what I mean.

Once I made a weekend retreat at a Carmelite Center. We were directed by the priests in charge to read and reflect on some of the writings of St. John of the Cross, notably his *Dark Night*. About sixteen women were in attendance, several of them married, a handful separated, and the rest single.

One woman stands out in my mind. Between conferences we had quiet periods for reading, walking and praying. Afternoons were free, and most took advantage of the beautiful grounds to get some exercise. On one of my walks I met this woman strolling alone, evidently in deep thought. We paced silently for a while and then struck up a conversation. I think of our encounter as similar to those brief but intimate exchanges one may share with a stranger on an airplane, in which we dare to risk being more personal because we will probably never see one another again.

I asked her why she was making this particular retreat. Her story turned out to be quite sad. Several months earlier she learned in the cruelest of ways that her husband was having a longstanding affair with another woman. His unfaithfulness crushed her completely. She considered herself a good wife and mother and could find no way to justify his infidelity. Her first reaction was to turn against him totally while they pursued by mutual agreement the painful process of legal separation. She was torn between love and hate. Her life was a mess. While she couldn't formulate it in these words, whatever a dark night was, she was in it. All of her goals seemed shattered. Nothing made sense anymore. Was it her? Was it him? Who was to blame? If he saw the light, could she forgive him and go on with her marriage, or would this cloud of suspicion hang on forever?

She sought the counsel of a trusted priest and together they explored her feelings, looking also at the part she might have played, however unwittingly, in her husband's unfaithfulness. One day the priest suggested that she read St. John's *Dark Night*. The text provided a real breakthrough. She did not profess to understand in any great depth what the mystical writer was saying, but she was deeply moved by his image of the dark night. It spoke to her soul. It seemed to mirror what she had been going through. She could see that one of the roots of her suffering was the fact that her pride had been hurt. She valued rather highly the image she created of being the perfect wife and mother. When her husband left her, she felt cheated not only of his love but of her self-image. St. John's text helped her to see that this image was really an obstacle to God's love. In some way the suffering she had gone through was His way of tempering her pride and bringing her closer to the truth of her dependency on Him, especially now that she had to endure loneliness. Slowly, she was trying to find ways in her heart to forgive her husband and wish him well.

She recalled an incident, humorous in its simplicity, to illustrate her point. About a week ago, when her husband came to take one of their sons to a football game, she offered to pack lunch for both of them. On the counter were two brown bags, two apples, some chocolate-chip cookies, lettuce, lunch meat and bread for the sandwiches. She was amused to find herself quite spontaneously putting in her husband's bag the lettuce that was less wilted, the meatier sandwich, the apple with the least brown spots, and the cookies with the most chips. Something or Someone inside her made her do this, she said. She really felt a wave of compassion going out of herself toward her husband. He may not have even noticed what he was eating, but for her it was a breakthrough moment. "There was something more loving than I, more generous and forgiving, at work in me that made me divide up the lunches in that way."

I was struck by this example and told her so. It was simple, yet real. It remained with me more than many so-called spiritual highs. God seemed to prefer this occasion to show her that giving the best apple to her husband was a sign of His love that alone can transcend human hurt and negativity. He took the bitterness out of her suffering. He made her see that inner transformation in Christ was more important than maintaining her false pride.

What did she intend to do after the retreat? For her it was a matter of continuing to comprehend what God was saying to her in this new situation. What did her separation mean in light of the Grand Formation Design we had been discussing? She sensed that the Lord was asking her to move to a new depth of transformation of heart. She wanted to become more humble, more open to others, less seeking of her own ego-perfection. She knew she had to appraise her inner attitudes before rushing to judge the limits of another.

Over the months she could notice some small but significant improvements in the quality of her spiritual life. She felt less angry, more gentle. She felt less inclined to escape in distracting activities, more able to welcome the alone times and the silence they afforded for reading and reflection. Strangely, she had thought she would become a closed, fearful person, but the opposite was true. Being single had helped her to be more open to other people, to accept her limits and thank God for the hidden gifts she was beginning to discover. She certainly felt less confined to former stereotypes of behavior and more able to explore her feelings. Still, she cautioned me not to get the impression that she was entirely content with her singleness. After years of marriage she had some unresolved problems to work out in the area of sexual intimacy. She trusted that in due time, by opening up to the reality of loving celibately, she would find a new range of satisfying relationships. Already she could detect a difference between her and her woman friends. For instance, in the past she would never have felt free to talk about these things to a relative stranger. Yet our encounter had been most helpful to her. She felt that as a single woman I could read between the lines. In this way, we were able to minister to one another.

I realize anew as I recall this experience how much our sense of being supported by a Mystery greater than we were drew us together. In our singleness we were able to acknowledge our utter insufficiency without this Divine, Loving Other. We evoked this sense of support in one another in serious conversation and later in much laughter. We could affirm for one another the importance of really letting go and letting God run our lives. Maybe we were strong women, but we knew from Whom our strength came. Though we experienced times of loneliness, we felt certain that our lives were growing richer in spiritual insight.

CIRCUMSTANTIAL SINGLES
MINISTERING TO ONE ANOTHER

In talking to persons who are single by circumstance, I find myself wanting to encourage them to open their hearts to others. It is much harder if one keeps these feelings bottled up inside. Other singles may be of great help to them. The disclosure of a possible call to singleness as a solitary life in the world does not happen by default. It has to come from within one's experience. One has to take a firm grip on one's life and make the most of it with manifest joyousness. It is a delight to meet a single person who is in tune with the abiding mystery of his or her life and willing to help others seek this transcendent experience.

Being single offers one an opportunity to celebrate life in a new way. One can focus on the limits of this condition, but it is more creative to discover its unique possibilities for spiritual formation. In the circumstance of singleness one can become an instrument of the Eternal, a messenger of divine meaning in the midst of human suffering. One can see in these unchosen limits the light of unique possibilities. To be in the circumstance of singleness thus calls for hidden heroism. One is thrust into the formation mystery that weaves through both the violent and gentle vicissitudes of time.

By reflecting prayerfully on the events that led to one's being single, one may uncover directives for the future that could not have been found otherwise. In this process feelings of insecurity, inadequacy and apparent meaninglessness may temporarily increase, but as one takes a more creative attitude toward these circumstances, new lights will emerge. For instance, it is possible that God is calling such a person to a special mission in the Church, however hidden or seemingly ordinary. Clearly the number of circumstantial singles is increasing. Separated and divorced persons are but one indicator. Who better than one who has gone through this experience can counsel those who are cast into the same darkness? Singles who have been separated from their spouses for a time can help those newly separated not to give up or lose their faith during this crisis period. They can help them to resist the tendency to banish this opportunity for a life review by losing themselves in frantic distractions. In a convinced way one can witness to the kind of faith that signifies peaceful surrender to God's will.

Being with others compassionately when they are in pain is one's way of showing that there is always some message to be found in suffering and human limitations if we take a moment to look for it. Being single by circumstance tests our capacity to love selflessly against the most challenging odds. Only if we can synchronize the pulse of faith with the beat of desperation can we tap into the creative energies of the spirit and expand our awareness of self, others and God. When something as major as singleness happens in one's life, we can be sure that it is not by mere happenstance. There is a reason for one's being single. The challenge of a lifetime is to discover what that is.

Suggested Readings

De Caussade, Jean-Pierre. *Abandonment to Divine Providence.* Trans. John Beevers. New York: Doubleday, Image Books, 1975.
   Abandonment to Divine Providence is one of the great Christian spiritual classics of all time. In it De Caussade emphasizes the total acceptance of the present moment as the single, most important concern of the soul seeking God. The present moment is "an ever-flowing source of holiness" for those who truly seek the Lord and His will in their everyday life situations.

Frankl, Viktor E. *Man's Search for Meaning: An Introduction to Logotherapy.* Trans. Ilse Lasch. New York: Washington Square Press, 1963.
   After three grim years at Auschwitz and other Nazi prisons, the author gained his freedom, only to learn that almost his entire family had been wiped out. During, and indeed partly because of, the incredible suffering and degradation of those years, he developed his theory of logotherapy which, in his own words, "makes the concept of man into a whole . . . and focuses its attention upon mankind's groping for a higher meaning in life."

John of the Cross. *The Collected Works of St. John of the Cross.* Trans. Kieran Kavanaugh, O.C.D., and Otilio Rodriguez, O.C.D. Washington, D.C.: ICS Publications, 1973.
   This one-volume edition offers the reader a new translation of *The Ascent of Mount Carmel, The Dark Night, The Spiritual Canticle* and *The Living Flame of Love,* including the poetry, of this great mystical doctor of our spiritual tradition. Each text unfolds St. John's intention to teach souls the dynamics of growth in union with God. He charts the course we must follow to achieve divine intimacy, from the active purification of our senses to the consummation of our whole being in perfect, participative union with the Holy Trinity.

Kazantzakis, Nikos. *Zorba the Greek*. Trans. Carl Wildman. New York: Simon and Schuster, A Touchstone Book, 1952.

The narrator spends six months working on the Cretan shore with the novel's hero, Zorba, an irrepressible Dionysian whose natural gusto for life is limitless. Through his most memorable character, Kazantzakis shows us the sunnier areas of the human spirit. The image of Zorba celebrating life and transforming even death into a dance touches the heart and imagination of modern readers.

Lewis C. S. *A Grief Observed*. New York: Bantam Books, 1976.

This book will be a comfort and an inspiration to anyone who has ever lost a loved one. These reflections express Lewis' doubts and rage at the loss of his wife after four happy years of marriage. Through the journal he moves from inconsolable loneliness and loss of belief in God back to life and on to an eloquent statement of rediscovered faith.

Lindbergh, Anne Morrow. *Gift from the Sea*. New York: Random House, A Vintage Book, 1965.

The setting of this highly acclaimed book is the seashore; the time, a brief vacation that uplifted the author from the distractions of everyday existence into the sphere of meditation. As the sea tosses up its gifts—shells rare and perfect—so the mind, left to its ponderings, brings up its own treasures of the deep. The shells (channelled whelk, double-sunrise, argonauta) become symbols for the aspects of life this active woman is contemplating: the restlessness, pressures and demands we face today; the hunger for leisure and silence; the call to inner peace and integration.

Thérèse of Lisieux. *The Autobiography of St. Thérèse of Lisieux: The Story of a Soul*. Trans. John Beevers. Garden City, N.Y.: Doubleday, Image Books, 1957.

This spiritual classic recounts the story of the saint's struggle to use her limitations in such a way as to reach the heights of sanctity. Writing as an act of obedience to her superiors, Thérèse tells in journal form the story of a simple, middle-class woman who, despite several physical, emotional and spiritual obstacles, lets God draw strength from her weakness, transforming her in His purifying love.

Vanauken, Sheldon. *A Severe Mercy*. New York: Harper & Row, Publishers, 1977.

This is a remarkable story of young love and marriage as told by the husband of Davy, whose death, while devastating him, also becomes an opening to new life and an affirmation of their mutual conversion to Christianity, thanks to the support and friendship of C. S. Lewis. This reminiscence offers one a stunningly beautiful text that both shatters and heals.

van Kaam, Adrian. *A Light to the Gentiles: The Life Story of the Venerable Francis Libermann.* Denville, N.J.: Dimension Books, 1959.
In this fully documented, universally relevant "psychobiography" of the founder of the Holy Ghost Fathers, the author has synthesized the multiple factors that guided Father Libermann's life. He suggests that we, too, must be prepared to allow our lives to unfold, step by step, through the various demands and influences that are given to us for the formation and realization of our fullest potential.

——. *Spirituality and the Gentle Life.* Denville, N.J.: Dimension Books, 1974.
This book is a collection of meditative reflections on the meaning of human gentleness and its role in our spiritual formation. It studies gentleness as a life-style, specifically as it relates to aggression and as it bears fruit in communion with the divine formation mystery.

——. "Provisional Glossary of the Terminology of the Science of Foundational Formation." *Studies in Formative Spirituality,* I, 3 (November 1980), pp. 449–79.
These terms pertinent to the science of foundational formation deal with the relative value of psychotherapy for appraising spiritual formation; the need for a theoretical synthesis of foundational formation; the basic causes of formation ignorance; and the ultimate aim of formation. In addition, the functions of the formative mind and will, with respect to appraising and choosing particular means of formation, are outlined.

4

****
****

Experiencing Limits
and New Horizons
as Single Persons

These words written to me in a letter from a single friend made quite an impression:

> I guess I've been single in my heart for as long as I can remember. Even as a child I can recall many instances when I felt myself standing at a distance from classmates or the neighborhood gang. It was not strange for me to go off by myself to walk or read or quietly sit looking at trees and flowers and birds. Though I also loved being with people, I must confess also to being a loner.
>
> This state never bothered me and even now I regard it as an early imprint of my later choice of singleness as a vocation. Even during high school and college I did not date that much. Marriage really did not interest me and I thought it was because I was too interested in study, in going to graduate school, in finding the area of professional service in which I could feel fulfilled.
>
> Now I realize that this lack of interest in dating or in making many efforts to meet Mr. Right was really

*due to my inmost call to the single life. I was and
am really happy to experience solitude and the silence that often accompanies it. I'm sure that I shall
need these extended moments of stillness for as long
as I shall live.*

How different her attitude is from those who see only the
limits of the single life. They lament that their outlets for socializing are narrow. They feel strange around married people
and imagine that their friends think of them as grist for the
matchmaking mill or as an emerging threat to couples whose
relationship is shaky. They say it is almost agonizing to attend
Church functions or community gatherings for singles because they feel as if those who come bear some kind of a
stigma. They report in themselves an unwitting "hunting" tendency, an at times uncontrollable instinct to check everyone
out as a possible mate. Worse than their hunting inclination is
the feeling of being hunted that pervades some of these group
sessions where men look *at* women and women pretend not to
look *at* men. It is an exceptional get-together where singles
can be with one another on a jovial, social basis with no mat-
ing atmosphere.

Just as unpleasant for many is the singles-bar scene. They
never really feel comfortable there, though by forcing themselves to make the effort they may once in a while have a
good time. Even though they don't like going out alone or
with the "boys/girls"—still, to sit at home night after night
with only the television for company is an appalling thought.
In desperation some may accept the first marriage offer that
comes along, only to find that they have leaped from the fry-
ing pan into the fire.

It saddens one to admit that such persons may never
have taken the time to reflect on the human and transcendent
possibilities of singleness. They have only beheld its limits
and taken flight from them. Cultural conditioning that is cou-
ple- or group-oriented may have prevented them from mak-

ing a commitment to the single vocation as productive and fulfilling in its own right.

To challenge these limited, detrimental assumptions about singleness, I want to suggest ways in which its limits open up new horizons of meaning—physical, functional and spiritual. The choice of a single vocation significantly affects Church and Society, for it opens up ample possibilities for creativity and service on the part of an increasing number of men and women.

PHYSICAL LIMITS AND POSSIBILITIES

Physically, every single person is a member of a family with a consequent genetic heritage. Imprinted upon us at birth is what Adrian van Kaam identifies as our "initial originality," that is, our given profile of likes and dislikes, the vital, temperamental, organismic substructure of our bodily being that will remain with us until death.[1] It is within the limits of this given body that subsequent functional-spiritual formation unfolds.

For instance, a temperament sensitive to nature may have within it the seeds of a highly developed capacity for solitude. A person with a weak physical constitution may find later that he or she does not have the energy required for family life, thus reading in one's body a possible call to singleness. Grace does build on nature. Before making any serious commitment, we must take time to appraise what our body has to tell us about our calling.

When this initial originality becomes actualized in daily life, van Kaam calls it "historical originality." The unique me, hidden in the to-be-formed regions of my initial self, is disclosed gradually as I grow and develop. I necessarily imbibe ethical and cultural customs, opinions and prejudices. How I deal with these, whether I accept them thoughtlessly

[1] Adrian van Kaam, *Living Creatively* (Denville, N.J.: Dimension Books, 1978), pp. 2–4.

or take a reflective stance toward them, has a great deal to do
with later vocational choices.

Is it not true that perhaps persons destined for singleness
have been pushed into marriage or religious life? A woman I
met at a Christian ministry conference confided, after my talk
on the single life, that she was one of those people who had
indeed been coerced into religious life by a stern father and a
devout mother, both of whom were determined that one of
their daughters would serve the Church as a sister. At the
time of her entrance into the community, the formation program was more regimented than personalized to meet each
one's questions and concerns. She accepted docilely whatever
she was told and after a time ceased trying to appraise her
own calling. She simply conformed to the community's expectations.

Following the upheavals in religious life after Vatican
Council II, and after months of serious spiritual direction, she
sought and was granted the proper dispensation. Yet she still
wonders at times if she made the right move in returning to
the world. This is a hard question to answer, but it is helpful
to recognize that historical influences exercise a powerful hold
on heart, mind and will. For that reason they must be carefully appraised at the time of making a serious decision pertaining to one's vocation.

FUNCTIONAL LIMITS AND POSSIBILITIES

Moving to the functional dimension of formation, we
may ask: What is it that prompts us to bring this initial originality to life in historical time and space? Van Kaam calls this
capacity for functional disclosure self-motivation or "operational originality." This is the power within us to embody
effectively in daily life our ideas and ideals—to move from
imagination to decision, from anticipation to action.

During young adulthood we relish the heady wine of
managing life and realizing ambitions. Our energy to function

well is doled out in nearly tireless performance. Our ability to remain productive without incurring the loss of altruism and the depletion of energy will depend on how well we temper these functional ambitions by transcendent aspirations. What van Kaam refers to as "social-presence erosion and depletion" is one of the chief dangers single professionals face, no matter what job or position they hold. They are inclined to work hard to realize their ideals without paying sufficient attention to their vital limits and transcendent aspirations.

Taking this caution into account, we must still stress that this operational component of originality is central for the single vocation. We need to live purposeful, creative lives oriented toward the pursuit of excellence in our profession and position and toward some kind of service to humanity that ties in with our temperament and talents. The single life can be demoralizing if it lacks this sense of higher functional fulfillment.

There is a special joy attached to excelling in some field or job, and the pursuit of this excellence ought to motivate singles to contribute to the culture without depleting themselves in the process. The opposite extreme is just as bad, namely, using singleness and its lack of family responsibility, suffering and sacrifice as an excuse for inertia. A young teacher I recall soon emptied out by flitting from one city to another instead of taking time to better herself educationally. In the same vein, I know a lawyer who is staying with a firm in a position that no longer challenges him because sheer complacency prevents him from seeking more fulfilling work.

By contrast, it should come as no surprise to singles if their pursuit of professional excellence arouses envy in some colleagues. One simply has to live with this reality. If it results in a feeling of loneliness, that too has to be expected. To think one can be a single, dedicated, skilled professional without occasionally arousing envy or feeling lonely would be naïve. Having encountered these two experiences frequently in my own life, I've come to accept them as normal challenges of the single state.

Active, dynamic, highly motivated yet content to be hidden and silently devoted—these qualities emerge as characteristic of healthy single functioning. I remember one of my college teachers, a single woman who taught in the science department. I'm sure she must have felt with the passage of years the pressure of routine. Sophomore biology students do not change that much. They flocked to her class because she always approached her lessons in a fresh manner, teaching enthusiastically and seeking new texts and examples. She revealed her love for the minutest forms of life, her delight in uncovering nature's hidden treasures.

Her influence on the students was always formative, for from her they received a living message pertaining to respect for creation. I hope that our voiced appreciation gave her something in return for her devotion—though her dignified self-confidence precluded the seeking of praise from her students. If it was given, fine, she accepted our gratitude graciously; if it was withheld, fine too. Her pursuit of excellence continued because the classroom to her was not just a place of learning but of love.

Another single friend of mine, a researcher and writer, may spend hours at his desk with little to show for his efforts. After a while, he tells me, his perseverance begins to pay off. Ideas click together; a concept he has been struggling to understand is suddenly clear. No one else may be there to notice it, but that hidden thrill of fresh insight compensates him for hours of routine reading and thinking. The fruits of his labors ripen in the book he is writing.

Still another single person, in this case a nurse, told me about one of her patients, an artist of some renown, who felt quite depressed in the sterility of his hospital room. One day, after work, she went to a neighborhood craft shop to look for something to brighten up his room. It took a few hours but finally she found the right gift, a charming arrangement of dried wild flowers in a shadow-box frame. The next day when she came into his room he was asleep. Quietly she hung the gift in eye's view. When he awoke, it was the first thing he saw. Later, with tears in his eyes, he thanked her for taking time to think of him and to enter into his esthetic sensibility.

Now he felt like a person and not merely a sick patient. She helped him to remember his original value, even in his illness and suffering.

When we give that extra touch of personal care beyond the call of duty, we tap into the creative potential hidden in us. An outstanding example is Dag Hammarskjöld, who served as Secretary-General of the United Nations. His spiritual diary, *Markings,* enables us to view the "negotiations" going on between him and God. Simultaneously, the records of history reveal his remarkable accomplishments in world diplomacy.

As a single person, Hammarskjöld realizes that a price must be paid if he is to follow God's call, reject duplicity for the sake of honest diplomacy, and serve humanity as a peacemaker. He senses that he has to give up the game of gaining popularity at any price and endure being lonely. In words that could serve as a code of ethics for single persons, he reminds himself:

> *The more faithfully you listen to the voice within you, the better you will hear what is sounding outside. And only he who listens can speak. Is this the starting point of the road towards the union of your two dreams—to be allowed in clarity of mind to mirror life and in purity of heart to mold it?*[2]

What he must listen to, if this dream is to become a reality, is not "the shouts and horns of the hunt," not the shrill cries of the crowd, but the hidden voice of the Lord.

SPIRITUAL LIMITS AND POSSIBILITIES

Not every single person can be a Dag Hammarskjöld, but the same principle of spiritual motivation applies to anyone

---

[2] Dag Hammarskjöld, *Markings,* trans. Leif Sjöberg and W. H. Auden (New York: Alfred A. Knopf, 1969), p. 12.

who aspires to a formation that places functional ambitions at the service of the Spirit. This service does not demand our getting involved in extracurricular activities. It sees as our first duty being present to God's call in the here-and-now situation. This is significant because there is a tendency in well-meaning singles to identify religious idealism with social-service projects; consciousness-raising rallies pointing to the plight of the poor and minority peoples; and fights for justice and equality. The importance of dedicated daily work may pale in comparison to these activities and make singles who are not called to such commitments feel guilty. Is second-grade teaching or office typing "great" enough in God's eyes?

It would be a grave error to give up one's compatible profession and respond wholly to these noble efforts out of false guilt feelings instead of a genuine inner call. Some may dedicate their single lives to service of the physically poor in slums, others to service of the spiritually poor on college campuses.

Where we serve and with what kind of graced motivation depends on an ongoing appraisal of our unique call. This appraisal begins in our hearts; it cannot be based on shifting cultural pressures. The works within which we can express our love for God and give witness to Christian values might range from scientific research to soup kitchens. We must not limit the Spirit to any one segment of the population but let It flow where It will. God values the small unnoticed duties of the present moment as well as feats of public acclaim, expressing social, artistic or scientific capability. The main question concerns not what we have done but how well we have found and developed in daily formation our hidden transcendent potential.

Another single person, the Danish philosopher Søren Kierkegaard, insists that when one appears before the Eternal, the Eternal is not interested in how many committees he or she has chaired or how popular was the cause one served. In his discourse entitled *Purity of Heart Is to Will One Thing*, Kierkegaard tells us that the Eternal asks only:

*Do you remember each time you throw yourself in
this way into the world around you, that in this relation, you relate yourself to yourself as an individual
with eternal responsibility? Or do you press yourself
into the crowd, where the one excuses himself with
the others, where at one moment there are, so to
speak, many, and where in the next moment . . .
there is no one? Do you judge like the crowd, in its
capacity as a crowd? You are not obliged to have an
opinion about what you do not understand. No, on
the contrary, you are eternally excused from that.
But you are eternally responsible as an individual to
render an account for your opinion, and for your
judgment. And in eternity, you will not be asked in-
quisitively and professionally as though by a newspaper reporter, whether there were many that had
the same—wrong opinion. You will be asked only
whether you have held it, whether you have spoiled
your soul by joining in this frivolous and thoughtless judging, because the others, because the
many judged thoughtlessly. . . . Eternity . . . never
counts. The individual is always only one and conscience in its meticulous way concerns itself with the
individual. In eternity you will look in vain for the
crowd.[3]*

In the light of these provocative words, we conclude that
being single can, by the very nature of this vocation, never
mean disappearing into the crowd and denying one's unique
call. Everyone eventually is going to be accountable before
the Eternal. Thus, listening to His voice is essential now.
Singleness means forming my life in openness to the Divine
Form and Image in whose love and light I am made. It means
being responsible to God's call and to the direction He gives

[3] Søren Kierkegaard, *Purity of Heart Is to Will One Thing*, trans.
Douglas V. Steere (New York: Harper Torchbooks, 1956), pp. 189–91.

to my single life—however limited this destiny may seem when measured by societal standards. To search for our foundational spiritual identity is everyone's responsibility on this earth, but it is a responsibility felt with special intensity by the single person.

LIVING IN TUNE WITH REALITY

As we have seen, singleness is regarded by many as a state to be freed from so one can be free for marriage. But for the *committed* single person, the opposite is true. He or she chooses to be freed from marriage so as to be free for the unique possibilities offered by the single vocation for personal and spiritual growth. Undoubtedly, being single does sharpen one's perception of the limits of life while simultaneously opening up new horizons of meaning.

We treasure our illusory idols, our unfulfilled expectations. To walk the razor's edge of the human condition is not the most comfortable position. Why can't we be either totally determined or totally free? Why must we live in the tension of situated freedom, of bound transcendence? Why must we kill expectations of life conforming to our will and wait upon the Lord? Pondering these eternal questions can evoke sadness, insecurity, fear and discouragement, yet to live in the questions, as single persons must, is to face life as it is, with all its ambiguity.

This option to live in tune with reality in a more reflective way has to be chosen at some point by single persons. They simply have more time to confront life's limits and possibilities than does the person committed to family or institutional life. This confrontation with reality happens in common ways. For instance, because there is no one face to whom the single person is bound by marriage, he or she may perceive more sharply the faces of other people. I walk along a busy street or sit observing travelers in a station, aware of the emotional scars on their lined faces. Life's limits are written there for one who takes time to read them. So too are life's small, fleeting joys as revealed in moments of reunion.

As I follow these life stories written in a face, I know that no matter how together a person may be or look, sooner or later one has to face the lonely limits of being a unique soul on this earth. The mask of confidence worn by that teenager will drop once the crisis of commitment is felt. Somewhere in that radiant young face lies the toothless grin of an old man just as that youth's buoyancy still lies asleep in him. Looking at them, the span of time between birth and death collapses into a brief moment.

Singleness as a chosen or accepted vocation has the effect of heightening one's perception of reality. The simple fact of waking up alone sets the tone for the entire day—again establishing limits but also revealing possibilities. True, we may talk to ourselves or turn on the television, but there is no one other person with whom to converse. And yet this same condition stimulates reflection. I have but *one* life to live. *Each* day has to count for something. What is the meaning of the *moment?*

In other words, heightened consciousness of time, its passing, its value versus its dissipation, strikes a haunting chord in our thought process. We strive to avoid a merely introspective, analytical, dissecting attitude. Singleness ought not to foster self-scrutiny but a more meditative approach to reflection. Such reflection facilitates growth in humility, for while appreciating one's autonomous possibilities, the reality of my being dependent on Another is also clear. St. Teresa of Avila's definition of humility is applicable here: to walk in the truth of who we are.[4] For me that means piercing through the illusion of total independence and admitting my ultimate need for God.

It is no good pretending to be anyone but who I am.

---

[4] *The Collected Works of St. Teresa of Avila*, trans. Kieran Kavanaugh, O.C.D., and Otilio Rodriguez, O.C.D., Volume Two (Washington, D.C.: ICS Publications, 1980), *The Interior Castle*, VI: 10, 7, p. 420.

When I try to "play the game" to the detriment of "walking in the truth," I end up being unhappy. For instance, I can now avoid empty socializing without feeling that there must be something wrong with me. I immensely enjoy socializing that means something: a fine conversation, dinner with friends, relaxed, accepting companionship. But I often feel drained out and condemned to keep a frozen smile when floating around at a cocktail party with strangers who seem desperately eager to "make it."

Idle chatter, gossipy exchanges, one-upmanship—these modes of relating make me long to return to my "hermitage," to go home alone and read a good book or listen to some music. Not that such occasions can always be avoided. Business makes them a necessity at times. For that reason, as a single person, I try to bring my hermitage with me in my heart. This "hermitage of the heart," as the spiritual masters call it, accounts in another way for the reflective stance typical of singleness.

Here, in the midst of surface noise, one can retire in reflective stillness. This stillness within creates just the right amount of distance, enabling me to be present where I am, even at the cocktail party, without being swept blindly into these party games. I experience a return to that rhythm of distance and nearness, thanks to the grace of inner silencing. I realize anew the significance of silence in my single life. Not only does it aid reflection; it also prepares me for my life of service.

Suggested Readings

Bossis, Gabrielle. *He and I.* Trans. Evelyn M. Brown. Sherbrooke, P.Q., Canada: Editions Paulines, 1980.
  He and I is the diary of a French woman, Gabrielle Bossis, in which are recorded the inspirations of the voice that guided and transformed her more and more during the last years of her life. When the hidden treasure of her unusual inner life becomes

known to her spiritual director, the Franciscan priest urges Gabrielle to become a nun. She resists his suggestion and remains a single woman in the world, as she feels interiorly impelled to do. Gabrielle wrote entertaining comedies, which she also produced and brilliantly acted. She died in 1950, while on an acting tour in Canada. Her testament of Christ's guidance and love speaks to each of us personally.

Kierkegaard, Søren. *Purity of Heart Is to Will One Thing.* Trans. Douglas V. Steere. New York: Harper & Row, Publishers, Harper Torchbooks, 1956.

In *Purity of Heart Is to Will One Thing,* Kierkegaard situates the "solitary individual" before God, lending an ultimate seriousness to the question of one's consciousness of individuality. Because one stands alone before God, each must answer Kierkegaard's searing questions: "What kind of life am I living? Do I, or do I not truthfully, sincerely, honestly, will one thing?" According to the author, the "solitary individual" pursues a life calling which recognizes the value of personal vocation and depends ultimately upon faith.

Brother Lawrence of the Resurrection. *The Practice of the Presence of God.* Trans. John J. Delaney. Garden City, N.Y.: Doubleday, Image Books, 1977.

Brother Lawrence's text is a classic example of the way in which an ordinary person can consecrate his or her life, however uneventful, totally to the ever-present God. It is based on the practice of ceaseless prayer, cultivated by a sense of the presence of God alive in every situation of our life.

Merton, Thomas. *The Sign of Jonas.* Garden City, N.Y.: Doubleday, Image Books, 1956.

A collection of personal notes and meditations set down during five years of Merton's life as a Trappist in the Abbey of Gethsemani, this spiritual diary records the difficulties and joys of someone struggling to let himself be drawn closer to the divine mystery of his life, a union promised to everyone through Christ's victory over suffering and death.

Steere, Douglas V. *On Being Present Where You Are.* Lebanon, Pa.: Sowers Printing Co., Pendle Hill Pamphlet #151, 1967.

The author seeks to discover in a series of interrelated reflections what it means to be present and what genuine presence implies. To be present can, on one level, mean to be located at a given point in space and time; but, more than this, it refers to the quality of being "all there"—bodily, mentally, spiritually, not living in "interior emigration." The author relates his remarks to the Quaker emphasis on prayer as an ever-available door by which to come into God's presence.

Teresa of Avila. *The Book of Her Life. The Collected Works of St. Teresa of Avila,* Volume One. Trans. Kieran Kavanaugh, O.C.D., and Otilio Rodriguez, O.C.D. Washington, D.C.: ICS Publications, 1976.
    Resembling a long letter, *The Book of Her Life* is Teresa's story of the mercy of God reaching out to the misery of every soul. The saint is certain that everyone is called to the summit of the mountain where only the glory of God dwells. She starts off by telling how from an early age she began to receive God's abundant graces, how she frustrated His work early in life and then surrendered to Him wholly within her soul. Her book is an extraordinary guide to the prayer of recollection and quiet.

——. *Interior Castle.* Trans. and ed. E. Allison Peers. Garden City, N.Y.: Doubleday, Image Books, 1961.
    Considered the most sublime and mature of Teresa's mystical writings, *Interior Castle* reveals the fullness of her experience in guiding souls toward spiritual perfection. Likening the soul to a castle with many rooms, she describes the various mansions through which it must pass in its quest for perfection before reaching the innermost chamber, the place of transfiguration and communion with God.

Van Breemen, Peter G. *As Bread That Is Broken.* Denville, N.J.: Dimension Books, 1974.
    The author delves deeply, yet simply, into the mystery of a God of love who loves us as His own, and whose profoundest desire is to share His life with us. This love of God, like the love and acceptance of other persons, enables us to become the unique persons God meant us to be. Our prayer is nothing less than our acceptance of God's love in total surrender to His will.

van Kaam, Adrian. *In Search of Spiritual Identity.* Denville, N.J.: Dimension Books, 1975.
    In Search of Spiritual Identity is a valuable resource book presenting the foundations of the spiritual life and the formative dimension of Foundational Catholic Spirituality. The text can be helpful to readers in quest of a more spiritual approach to everyday living, especially through a mode of self-presence that is meditative and transcendent rather than analytical and introspective.

——. *Living Creatively*. Denville, N.J.: Dimension Books, 1978.

The author of *Living Creatively* presents a rich study of the complexities involved in living one's originality in a culture oriented toward conformity. While living a more creative life, self-motivated persons, who discover and attempt to embody in the world their ability to be themselves in a unique way, will frequently meet with destructive envy in others. This book is a source of encouragement for all who seek to live up to their Christian call and aspire to transcendent living in a functional society.

——. "Provisional Glossary of the Terminology of the Science of Foundational Formation." *Studies in Formative Spirituality*, II, 1 (February 1981), pp. 117–43.

This issue distinguishes the incarnational-directive sources of human and Christian formation (i.e., formative memory, formative anticipation and formative imagination). They are incarnational insofar as they assist mind and will in their task of directing the concrete incarnation of transcendent ideals in daily life.

5

✣✣✣✣✣✣✣✣✣✣✣✣✣✣✣
✣✣✣✣✣✣✣✣✣✣✣✣✣✣✣

Silence,
Compassionate Service
and the Single Life

Despite the noise pollution of modern times, the impact of the media and the thoughtless abuse of nature, human beings—single or otherwise—remain seekers of silence. This is so because of our transcendent nature. We seek that *more* beyond words which only silence can contain. Silence facilitates the opening of our hearts to that *other* beyond ourselves, to the Divine. All of nature, ourselves included, is drawn into this silence. A mysterious presence forms our life from birth to death and beyond death in the silent mystery of the eternal.

This connection with the transcendent may account for the profound attraction many singles feel for silence—at least a certain amount of it daily. It is linked, of course, to the single person's life of solitude, which inevitably provides more quiet space and time.

The danger is always there that singles will retreat into silence as a defensive posture. A maiden aunt of mine used the "silent treatment" as an excuse for not coping with her fear of people. At times she even refused to talk, because she was afraid of saying the wrong thing and having to cope with the consequences.

Too much silence, if a person is unsound psychologically, can be a breeding ground for mental illness. People live in self-enclosed prisons and lose the art of gracious communication. Given this danger, of which singles must be aware, can we propose a more positive approach to silence? Can we find a relation between it and compassionate service?

SILENCE AND SPEECH

A renowned philosopher, Max Picard, says in his book *The World of Silence* that language becomes emaciated if it loses its connection with silence.[1] Silence protects speech and enables it to become a communication of what is true and good. It prevents conversation from degenerating into chatter. In one of his books, *Thoughts in Solitude*, Thomas Merton calls silence the mother of truth.[2] It helps us to refocus our scattered attention and consequently to say thoughtful things.

Lacking silence, life takes on a buckshot approach. Our mind starts racing, distractions abound. We can hardly hold on to one thought before another comes rushing in. Silence stills this inner disquiet and enables us to recollect ourselves around a center of meaning. It helps us to focus on our worries, anxieties and fears, and to begin to diffuse them. That can and does happen if we welcome silence as a healing experience.

However, if we are afraid of silence as such, it can be threatening. Nothing seems worse than to face the noise inside us, so we make sure that there is plenty of noise outside us. We turn on the television or radio, get on the phone, talk to the four walls—anything to escape the silence. If we can get past this fear of hearing or saying nothing, then once again silence can become a welcome friend that fosters recollection and readies us for meaningful speech and action.

Silence becomes a sanctuary of reflection and prayer, an answer, as it were, to our deepest needs, a dimension of tran-

[1] Max Picard, *The World of Silence*, trans. Stanley Godman (South Bend, Ind.: Gateway Editions, 1952), p. 15.
[2] Thomas Merton, *Thoughts in Solitude* (New York: Doubleday, Image Books, 1968), p. 84.

scendence. In those silent moments singles enjoy at the beginning and end of the day, stress, confusion and agitation disappear. Peace and rest invade one's heart and mind. We can breathe a sigh of relief and ready ourselves for the next day's demands.

Silence serves speech in another sense. We know from experience that words often betray what we really intend to say. In our minds the point we want to make is perfectly clear. We formulate interiorly just the right combination of words, but they come out of our mouths all wrong. It would have been better to remain silent. Then, too, when we lack the protection of inner silence, our words can burst forth impulsively and hurt people. What we say in anger comes back to shame us. We would give anything to retract our words and try again.

It is also true that some experiences between people transcend the boundaries of language. Think of exquisite moments of love and trust between friends. They cannot find words to articulate what they are feeling, nor do they want to. What is happening between them is beyond words. It calls only for a silent exchange, perhaps complemented by a quiet visual beholding, a touch of the hands, a gentle smile.

These silent gestures are so much richer than words right now. We are simply present in silence to one another, yet a vast amount of communication is going on. Something in us has been drawn upward at that moment into the realm of mystery. Maybe we are experiencing the Sacred. Maybe we are in touch with that silent treasure that resides in the core of our being.

SILENCE AND PRESENCE

Silence also denotes a deep quality of presence in which we may sense the nearness of God. It is formative of the interior life and a must for the single vocation. We cannot really be single, in my opinion, unless we can live with and enjoy silence and solitude. The bond between our human spirit and the Divine Spirit is silence; the love that binds us in our aloneness to the Alone is solitude.

Perhaps we could rephrase the directive of the psalmist: "Pause a while and know that I am God" (Ps. 46:10) to say: Be silent and let go of all inner strife. Clear the mind of its many worries. Listen to the hushed whisper of God in our hearts. Know that silence touches every sphere of existence, leading us ultimately to the adoration of the Lord.

Silence brings to our bodies the grace of relaxation, to our minds increased attention. It makes possible thoughtful speech and leads to more reflective action. It helps us most of all to be centered in God. If we do not nourish our souls in silence and solitude, they shall atrophy as bodies do without food. Silence and solitude, by stilling our minds and hearts, ready us for those moments when God draws us to Himself in a union of intimate love.

Can we not conclude that the atmosphere of stillness in which His word can be heard is rooted in silence; that the space in which we can reflect on its meaning is created by silence; that the heart which can be touched, because it opens itself vulnerably to God, is softened through silence?

Ultimately, it is only silence that can contain any direct experience of God. To attain this state is not a matter of willful forcing but of patient letting go. It was Franz Kafka who once observed:

You do not need to leave your room. Remain sitting at your table and listen. Do not even listen, simply wait. Do not even wait, be quite still and solitary. The world will freely offer itself to you to be unmasked, it has no choice, it will roll in ecstasy at your feet.[3]

[3] Franz Kafka, *The Great Wall of China: Stories and Reflections* (New York: Schocken Books, 1946), p. 307.

This still point is disclosed only in surrender, in daily dying, in relinquishing our ego projects as ultimate. At the center of this solitude we may experience oneness with God. It is our personal need for silence as singles that should prompt us to set aside times and places of quiet presence to facilitate inner stilling and aloneness before the Lord.

We can adopt the attitude of shifting the center of our focus from worldly concerns to God alone. Humbly and serenely returning to this inner state of quiet assures that we can be with Him any time of the day or night. In silence we simply love the Lord—and the deeper our love is, the fewer words it needs.

SILENCE AND SERVICE TO OTHERS

The inner stilling that fosters reflection energizes the single person for service. Certainly one's mode of service, one's career choice, is an important factor in fostering a single vocation. If we can approach our work as a form of ministry, what we do becomes an expression of who we are as servants of the Sacred. Work is not reduced to empty routine, the aim of which is remuneration. It becomes an ennobling opportunity to give of ourselves to others and to promote the common good of humanity. Such concerns must be uppermost in our minds as we enter the work force and increase our professional competence. In short, singles need a sense of ministry if their work is to become a mode of care and not merely a means of making more money.

Perhaps the deepest meaning of a single person's service is this orientation to otherness. The opposite of this orientation poses a tremendous obstacle to our living a spiritual life as single persons, namely, a narcissistic pursuit of self-gratification that kills generosity.

Many books written today address the increasing number of people who are living alone, but their underlying theme, echoing the general trend toward secularization in culture, stresses how great this life is because it maximizes the freedom to be ourselves, to do exactly what we feel like doing, to become wholly self-reliant. *Self* is an oft-used word in single-life books. Spirituality hardly appears, and otherness, if mentioned, usually means what others can do for me.

This corrosive emphasis on self in isolation from others and God makes the single life seem like the final solution of the Me Generation. Its aim becomes to make Glorious Me as perfect as possible: poised, in control of my sexuality, not dependent ultimately on anyone but myself, capable of scheduling every day to suit my desires. It goes without saying how detrimental such attitudes are to the life of the spirit. Unless we silence these narcissistic voices, single life risks destroying the transcendent orientation that gives it its reason for being.

We must recognize as singles the ever-present danger of egocentrism. Perhaps the best and only way of tempering it is by this orientation to otherness that is at the base of our capacity to be of service. The horizon of this orientation extends ultimately to the Divine Other in whom our aloneness finds its fulfillment in transforming oneness.

A true grace of being single is that it disposes us toward this sacred bond with God. We know that in our uniqueness, we reach out for union. Self alone can never satisfy our longing to belong to Another. The single person does not lose this longing because he or she is not married. If anything, the longing increases because one knows that even in marriage it cannot be satisfied. As Psalm 42 expresses it, the soul longs for God as a doe longs for running streams to slake its thirst. No one can ever satisfy this yearning—no one but the Divine Other.

In the meantime, some spiritual satisfaction can come through a giving of self to others in service. Without going into practical details, dependent on each work situation, we can suggest some principles of responsible service on the part of singles. First of all, respect for the uniqueness or ultimate singleness of others. In our service we can respond to a basic need in others to feel worthwhile and respected in their own right. We can resist imposing upon them our own image of who they are and try to draw out the unique image of God in which they are made.

Secondly, the creation of welcoming space. Singles can create around them a nonmanipulative space where others really feel comfortable being themselves. The creation of this atmosphere is rooted in what Adrian van Kaam calls "formative benediction."[4] This word derives from the Latin term which means to "speak well." Benediction is a formative experience, whether we bless others or receive a blessing from them. It comes in the form of an inner or outer word or gesture arising from a loving heart. In blessing we express gratitude to God for the divine form inherent in other persons. We ask God in effect to bring this form to its fullness. Heartfelt benediction is basic to effective formation between persons, and hence it becomes a major goal of single service. Any number of people who cross our path need such a blessing, whether we express it by just listening to them or by offering an encouraging word.

Thirdly, the increase of compassion. Compassion is, of course, a foundational disposition to be practiced no matter what one's chosen vocation may be. For the single person it is probably the best protection we have against the obstacles of narcissism, solipsism, withdrawal and self-sufficiency—all of which belie the vulnerable nature of the human condition. We could describe compassion as a way of seeing the world with eyes that behold its pathos and joy. It lessens our preoccupation with power, pleasure and possession and enables us to see beneath the surface of things to a deeper, transcendent meaning.

SINGLENESS AND COMPASSIONATE SEEING

Compassionate seeing is the opposite of analytical, removed observation. It participates in the widest possible

---

[4] Adrian van Kaam, "Formative Benediction" in "Provisional Glossary of the Terminology of the Science of Foundational Formative Spirituality," *Studies in Formative Spirituality*, I, 1 (February 1980), p. 146.

range of human emotion and potential. There may not be the slightest exchange between myself and another—not even eye contact—and yet in that figure, slumped by life's limits or elated by its possibilities, I behold myself and all people. This seeing teaches me lessons not to be learned in books. The wrinkled old woman, fragile and alone in her hospital room, seen with compassion, is my teacher. She is a living lesson pertaining to the aging process each of us must undergo in our singularity. That old gentleman in the park evokes compassionate seeing. He teaches me through his benevolent smile that life becomes increasingly uncomplicated as we near death. For each of us it is reduced to essential things, what makes us most sad or most happy. Maybe for him a letter from his son, a glass of sherry with friends at the local pub, a chance to sit and feed the pigeons.

When I really see a pert three-year-old, intent upon a butterfly or soaring free with his flying kite, I'm struck by the eternal promise of youth: undaunted, imaginative, formed as a unique expression of the divine playfulness. These figures and myriad others speak to me of the mystery of singularity and evoke gratitude for my vocation.

The more I live in compassion, the more I see through my egoism and its prideful trappings. The more I empty my heart of selfish desires, the more clarity of sight I gain. This slow emergence of compassionate seeing not only directs me toward others; it also enables me to see myself with new eyes. Before I might have seen my single state as a separate entity, as a lonely self having to fight for survival in a world where others cared little about me. It was easy then to buy into slogans like "control or be controlled," "win whatever the cost." What was life but a battlefield where only the fittest could survive? The rule was: Be more successful, more efficient, more clever than the next person. The pressure escalated to keep producing and proving myself. All of this resulted in anything but a spiritual vision of who I was as a single person.

Compassionate seeing changes the way I look. With eyes open to the Eternal, I cease to regard myself as a separate entity, standing alone against the rest of the world. The world is not only a collection of resistances to be overcome but a mystery evocative of wonder. Compassion makes me feel part of all that is because everything shares a common source. I realize vividly the omnipresence of God's Forming Mystery. He is everywhere and in everything. He wills our well-being. Wherever we go, wherever we are, we find Him as the deepest source of formation in His creation while infinitely transcending it. We feel inwardly free knowing that we are being drawn into the depths of His love, a love that may be invisible to the eyes of the world but that is wholly visible to the eyes of faith. Such is the gift of compassionate seeing.

The wondrous, in contrast to the resistant, response corrects my vision of singleness. No longer do I view myself as a lonely entity in a world cut off from God and other people. I see myself and others as held by the Holy, as loved into being, as part of His forming plan of creation and redemption.

Where before I saw fragmentation and fight, I now see communion and reconciliation. Such a view of ultimate oneness with nature, others and God may dim momentarily when pressures mount, but through silence and prayer I can place myself once again in His caring presence. Behind the tempest I behold the cloudless night. Beneath the turbulence of the sea is the calm of the ocean's floor. Here I can rest in God and regain my inner strength, lost through worldly dissipation and proud forgetfulness.

The grace God gives me to regain compassionate seeing calls for my cooperation. It asks again and again that I diminish self-centered desires and become a more patient person, ready to see and follow His divine directives in day-to-day encounters. The person who radiates the compassionate glow of God's love is bound to be beheld by others as singular. Through faith and love our heart goes out to others. Our compassionate look tells all, for it cuts through loneliness and enables others to behold in us the loveliness of the Lord.

Suggested Readings

Carretto, Carlo. *Letters from the Desert*. Trans. Rose Mary Hancock. Maryknoll, N.Y.: Orbis Books, 1972.

Born of the author's solitude and contemplation as a Little Brother of Jesus in the desert country of North Africa, these reflections stand well within the ancient Christian tradition of desert experience, allowing the thoughtful reader an opportunity for encounter with self, God and others in silence and compassion.

——. *In Search of the Beyond*. Garden City, N.Y.: Doubleday, Image Books, 1978.

The author finds the source of his prayer in the solitude and harshness of the Sahara, where each day becomes an act of faith. Few of us have the occasion for such isolation, but he insists that we would benefit greatly by creating a desert in our lives to which we would regularly withdraw to pray. Carretto becomes a trusted guide and companion for each reader in this search for the beyond.

Dunne, John S. *The Reasons of the Heart: A Journey into Solitude and Back Again into the Human Circle*. New York: Macmillan, 1978.

A powerful description of the hard, but hopeful, road from loneliness to love, Dunne's journey into the human heart begins with the loneliness of the human condition. He shows the reader how, by embracing solitude, persons come to know themselves and the path they are meant to pursue. By coming to themselves in solitude, they also come to others and then to God. The heart's search does not end in solitude but returns again into the human circle.

Maloney, George A. *Inward Stillness*. Denville, N.J.: Dimension Books, 1976.

This book is an invitation to accept God's call issued in Psalm 46: "Be still and know that I am God." Its main theme is the mystery of deeper communication with God, illumined by insights from Eastern Christian writers on the "prayer of the heart." Insights are also drawn from the Far East as well as from modern psychology and the whole area of expanded consciousness to present a form of deep interior prayer that can lead us into God's mystery and help us to become better human beings. The author presents prayer as a continual process of inner healing that allows us to live in God's "uncreated energies" and to pray incessantly as we find God in our own human situation.

Merton, Thomas. *Thoughts in Solitude*. New York: Doubleday, Image Books, 1968.
Like his *Seeds of Contemplation, Thoughts in Solitude* is a book of meditations for all thoughtful Christians. Merton speaks of the person's inalienable right to solitude and interior freedom as the safeguard of true human society. Through interior solitude persons in all sectors of society can reach a sense of personal integrity and the courage to give themselves to the future of religion and the world.

Picard, Max. *The World of Silence*. Trans. Stanley Godman. South Bend, Ind.: Gateway Editions, 1952.
The World of Silence is a celebration of silence in a noisy world, a theme all persons in our century can appreciate. Picard contends that silence is a basic value that defies the worlds of profit and utility. In silence one is healed and made whole again, restored on a deeper level to the spiritual meaning of persons, things and events.

Thoreau, Henry David. *Walden*. New York: Lancer Books, 1968.
First published in 1854, *Walden* is an incisive account of one man's attempt to experience nature firsthand and to penetrate beneath it to the mystery of its transcendent Source. Thoreau was twenty-eight years old when he moved to Walden Pond on July 4, 1845. There, for two years, he remained alone, reduced his needs to the barest essentials, and ate only food he could gather or grow. The eighteen essays describe his experiences of self-reliance, economy, silence and solitude, and his ever-expanding interest in spiritual growth. "Man flows at once to God," writes Thoreau, "when the channel of purity is open."

van Kaam, Adrian. "Provisional Glossary of the Terminology of the Science of Foundational Formation." *Studies in Formative Spirituality*, II, 2 (May 1981), pp. 291–328.
These glossary entries deal with the reduction of the meaning of science and of the scientific method, partial-pragmatic formation sources, formative social conscience and consciousness, and formative social peace.

Waddell, Helen, trans. *The Desert Fathers*. Ann Arbor, Mich.:
The University of Michigan Press, 1957.

The desert has bred fanaticism, frenzy and fear, but it has also
bred heroic gentleness and a transformed life of prayer. The
words of those quiet men who in the fourth century founded the
desert rule are here translated and introduced with a vivid description of the rich solitude of the desert.

Ward, Sr. Benedicta, trans. *The Sayings of the Desert Fathers:
The Alphabetical Collection*. Kalamazoo, Mich.: Cistercian Publications, 1975.

This translation makes accessible in English the sayings of the
Desert Fathers, previously available only in fragments. The wisdom of the desert speaks directly to all those who understand
that in one way or another the time for rendering accounts is
upon us. To meditate on that wisdom is to enter an eternal dimension. From their unrelenting courage, from their vision of
God, the Desert Fathers possessed such a love that nothing less
than their whole being could respond to it. If we wish to understand their sayings, we must approach them with veneration, silence our judgments and thoughts, and meet them on their own
ground. Only then can we hope to emulate the earnestness, de-
termination and infinite compassion of their silent communion
with God.

6

****
****

Singles Being with
and Caring for Others

I sense in my solitude that I am, that all things and people are, a sharing in the formative outpouring of God's love. Nothing I can be or make or do comes from me alone. All is but a sharing in the abundant Source. As God has shared Himself generously with us, so must we share with one another.

A single person's life would be empty of meaning and subject to delusion were it not shared with others. This sharing can take many forms. It may at times mean giving away some of our goods and possessions. Equally important is a sharing of ideas and ideals. For instance, most singles I know relish the sharing of thoughts and beliefs in a stimulating conversation. To cultivate this art can lead to a refined mode of relating, to a building of mental and spiritual bonds that reflect our appreciation of one another.

The sharing of ideals, as with professional colleagues, can draw singles into a kind of support association. We bind our time and talents to a common service while respecting one another's unique gifts. In my experience, dedicated single persons can function excellently in a team. They are accustomed to listening to others as well as to giving of themselves.

This capacity for self-gift forms and sustains a support

association. In practice this kind of group does not require in any way that the members live a common life as in a religious congregation, nor does it mean that they bind themselves through vows as in secular institutes. After all, what distinguishes this vocation from the latter choices, as well as from marriage, is one's status as a single person alone in the world. Singles can live without the support of such an association, but should something along these professional lines emerge, it does promote a sharing of ideas and ideals.

Whether in one's place of employment or with family or friends, the principle remains that singles do need to feel some support for their commitment. Though they live alone and strive for financial independence, they are not only "loners." They need and appreciate understanding and encouragement. A single Christian, to take but one case, living in a secularized culture may find it difficult to maintain Christ-centered values. It helps to hear that others affirm our commitment and encourage us to talk about it. It hurts to have to remain silent all the time or to feel that others put us on the defensive. Our vocation, though rigorous in its demands, offers us great joys, and we want to share them.

Some may try to exploit this need by capitalizing on the free time singles have. This happened to me once when I worked for a local publishing firm. The editor made me feel that I should always be the one to volunteer for the evening shift because, unlike himself and the others on the staff, I had no family for whom to care. He used subtle tactics like reminding me of the time I seemed to have on my hands because I was single. He tried to make me feel guilty if I said no to extra activities like collecting for his favorite charity.

It may be equally tempting to make singles feel guilty if they do not stop everything and help support the projects of friends or family members, whether one feels at home with them or not. I once knew a girl who was crazy about crafts. She joined three or four different guilds and couldn't understand why I refused to accompany her to these meetings. If we were really friends, she coaxed, then I should try to share her interests. It never seemed to occur to her to share mine. Such conditional offers of friendship demand a second look before one gets involved against his or her better judgment.

The friendships that last seem to emerge as part of God's providential plan for one's life. These persons are responsive to our likes and dislikes; they become helpmates in the formation process He wills. Such friends and colleagues freely come together for work and leisure without compulsion or coercion. If unforeseen circumstances separate them, they can leave this circle blessed by one another, consoled by the knowledge that spiritual ties can never be severed.

In this way, single persons remain alone while sharing themselves with many others. Such sharing can flower in an atmosphere where each one's ideas and ideals are welcomed and supported.

CARING FOR OTHERS AS SINGLE PERSONS

That we humans can triumph over initial narcissism and reach out to care for others is itself a spiritual victory. To care is, therefore, characteristic of being human as such. It signifies the priority humans give to the power of interformation, that is, to the condition of being with and for others. Human life is made up of such we-relationships. From the first moment of life to the last, though we are alone, we are also in some way in contact with others. Without fellowship no unfolding of the human species would be possible. This capacity to care accounts for the preservation of life and the environment that sustains it.

We mention these obvious facts to counterbalance any notion that singleness is maintained at the expense of caring relationships. The opposite is true: only to the degree that one fosters caring relations with others can one dare to risk being single. To make self the center of the universe is an ever-present danger for single persons. This egocentric posture is the antithesis of what it means to live a harmonious, spiritual single life. For this reason, singles ought to exemplify what it means to care for others, to respect them in their uniqueness, to foster their congenial formation.

Singles ought to be involved daily in the ministry of care. How is this ministry lived concretely? Taking as a clue the second part of the Great Commandment (to love my neighbor as I love myself), we can say that caring for others must include loving and respecting oneself.

By self we do not mean the proud, functional ego, operating at the expense of others, but the true self formed in the image and likeness of God and open to the highest spiritual values like trust, fidelity, generosity. When I love myself, it means that I love who I really am: a limited creature called to limitless joy; a fallible, finite being who can transcend sinful inclinations and seek the Infinite. It is this deepest self, this miracle of nature and grace, that I must esteem as a single person.

Just as we nourish our bodies with proper food and drink, so must we take care of this transcendent dimension of our lives. We strive to be attentive to all levels of personhood in this light: to our feelings and to what it is that generates a wide range of moods and emotions; to our ambitions and aspirations; to the directives inspired by the Holy Spirit and appraised in one's life situation. To attend to these levels of life, with all their implications for harmonious formation, is a lasting commitment of the single person. Only when we care for the self that we are, in light of the formative mystery, can we care for fellow selves in solicitous, responsible interformation.

MISCONCEPTIONS PERTAINING TO THE CARE OFFERED BY SINGLES

Before suggesting some avenues of care, I think we should clear up a few misconceptions. Singles have to break through the myth of total availability and the "slave" status it tends to generate. To be a servant of others is not to be a slave to their whims. I mention this because family members, friends, students, patients, colleagues, even strangers, are tempted to use single persons for their purposes because they are not married or responsible to an outside organized community.

Part of the problem of reducing the single person to slave status has to do with the fact that there are no symbolic rituals surrounding this vocation and thus setting its limits clearly before others. An elaborate ritualization engulfs the couple from the time of their engagement to the day of marriage and thereafter during the honeymoon period. From backyard ceremonies to the Royal Wedding in the summer of 1981, marriage is protected as a distinct style of life by ritual.

This ritual speaks symbolically of the new exclusivity of the married couple. Now they are responsible first and foremost to one another and to their potential family. They are not as free for other family members nor for community service as they were prior to marriage. The tendency is to leave them alone to start their own life. Wise parents cease to make demands on their time. Many small rituals continue to set the couple apart and give them a new identity. Now it is their apartment, their car, their kind of cooking and so on. Such rituals make it clear to others that their privacy is to be respected.

Similarly, the rituals surrounding ordination to the priesthood or the profession of final vows in a religious community or secular institute provide the person, through the power of symbol, with a marked identity. Parents treat the priest (their son) or the sister (their daughter) with the respect due their state in the Church. They relinquish them into the larger service of the human family in a parish, school, hospital, social-service association or whatever. The way they spend their time comes under the jurisdiction of a ritualized style of life. Even if the rituals change with the times, a sense of their identity is still symbolically secured.

Not so for the single person in the world. Even now, despite the increasing numbers of people living this state of life, despite the growing number of books and articles on the subject of singleness, society has no rituals designated to support this vocation in the world. It is truly hidden. Who sends out invitations to celebrate one's son's or daughter's choice of singleness? What newspaper clipping and photo proudly announce this decision? Mostly and by preference, the choice of a single vocation is made and lived out in relative, nonritualized hiddenness.

However, some people—often those in the family circle—even with the best of goodwill simply assume that this single state does not have its own autonomous rights but means being "available" for them. It is tempting to make a single person feel guilty for needing time alone in silence and solitude. A thoughtless response to false guilt can trap one in the myth of total availability as a defensive posture, that is, compelling singles to defend their worthwhileness by never saying no to the demands of others.

Though this vocation is not ritualized, we insist that it does have rights, and one of these is the right to privacy and time alone for silence, reading, reflection, prayer, recreation. If these rights are respected, then singles can follow their call to care for others without risking the erosion and depletion of their social presence. Of course, singles do have more time for others—this is one of the privileges of their vocation. But, by the same token, they need more time for inner resourcing.

Who is not grateful to that teacher who can spend extra time after school or on weekends helping her students? Or to that nurse who can forgo watching the clock and sit after official work time with a patient in need? This extra time is freely given and ought to be as freely received. One must not build expectations that it will always be there.

The single person who takes responsibility for a demanding ministry also needs a lot of time to reflect and pray, to study and write, to seek further education to promote professional excellence. Singles often display a highly developed esthetic sensibility and for this reason need to participate in cultural activities that keep alive their interest in art and music. Any leveling of this esthetic component in a false effort to be "in with the gang" or one of the "regular guys" can be devastating.

Singles are, like it or not, somewhat different from the rest of the population. Why would theirs be a unique vocation were this not true? If a single person betrays his or her inmost creative self, the result is usually some form of depression. Thus, it may take a lot of extra time—time away from friends, family members, crowds and colleagues—to simply cope with one's sensitive temperament and continually reset one's priorities in response to God's call.

How many times a single person will see and feel things others never notice. This sensitivity creates a certain inner intensity that again takes time to calm down and assimilate into the general demands of daily life. And yet, people caught up in the swirl of family and community activities, or overly influenced by various pressures in the culture, can be insensitive to the plight of the single person. They tell John not to brood so much over nothing and to go out and volunteer his time to help the less fortunate. They warn Mary to snap out of her moods and go help her parents clean house. They question Sarah's need to be alone so much and can hardly resist the tendency to invade her privacy.

Again, many of these problems may be traceable to the nonritualized nature of the single state. The important thing is that the single person be comfortable when misunderstanding occurs, while at the same time quietly resisting such a leveling mentality. There is nothing wrong with John or Mary or Sarah. They are just being single!

RESISTING THE WORKAHOLIC PHENOMENON

Often single persons, in order to justify their existence, begin to work themselves to death. In an achievement-oriented society like our own, almost everyone lauds these prodigious labors. No matter if the single person is a wreck physically, "that fellow/gal is the best worker we've ever seen."

I once knew a doctor who preached to his patients the need for eight hours' rest, eight hours' work, eight hours' leisure a day—truly a balanced program that he himself, a single man, never lived. Instead, he worked eighteen hours or more a day, dying in his late forties.

No one would undermine the adage: A good day's work for a good day's pay. Nor would we want to lose the readiness to work above and beyond the call of duty. Zeal and dedication are inspiring qualities in any profession. But there is a limit to how much we can work without losing the capacity for leisure and rest.

It is easy to lose this balance if one is single—and to err on the side of work much more than on that of recreation or sufficient sleep. Someone coyly remarks: "It must be nice to go wherever you want whenever you want to." Despite the fact that this is a thoroughly unrealistic statement, a swift pang of guilt may be felt by the single person, prone already to take on more work as a defensive measure. The result may be to try to outwork everyone, to show them what I can do if I set my mind to it.

Being in competition with oneself on the level of productivity is not only exhausting personally; it also makes it difficult to be present to others in an inspired, compassionate way. People are likely to dismiss us as fanatics or, worse still, to place us on a pedestal out of reach of ordinary people. In either case, we are left alone, even if we don't want to be.

Thus, as a single person, I must give fully of myself to those for whom I am professionally and socially responsible—for instance, students, patients, counselees, colleagues. I must even be willing to exert myself above the call of duty for a good cause or in the use of my talents. However, I cannot neglect the values of proper rest and recreation, of the repletion of my inner resources, in accordance with my interests and needs.

Life has to be scheduled to a degree, but not too rigidly. I cannot get to the point where my work allows for "zero flexibility" where other nonfunctional needs are concerned. There are times when I have to respect the call to cease doing and simply be. These being-times are not "nothing states," for in them a lot of inner, preconscious activity is going on. Here proceeds the work of creative reflection. Here disparate thoughts coalesce into new constellations of meaning. These are the times that restore me interiorly so I can indeed give fully of myself to others.

SINGLES SHOWING CARE

We can only care for others in committed service when we temper availability and avoid depleting overwork. In other words, our saying no to people at certain times must be for the sake of a greater yes. It is for this reason that I would like to suggest some ideals of caring toward which a single person may aspire.

What comes to mind first of all is the importance of taking time to listen to others. This involves disciplining the tendency to "jump the gun," or to "have the last word." We try to listen carefully to the questions others have and to give them a reflective answer. It is amazing how many people are capable of working through their own problems if they can just find someone who will take a few minutes to listen to them.

Secondly, the single person through reflection, dedicated efforts and much prayer ought to assume responsible leadership whenever and wherever possible, provided, of course, that such a position is congenial with one's talents, skills and temperament. He or she should be the type of person others call forth for such a position. To be a humble, devoted leader grants the single person a profound sense of inner fulfillment. One knows that the effects of this caring service will extend beyond the immediate situation and in some small or greater way create a better world.

A single person must, thirdly, live and witness to the way of moderation or following the "golden mean." I mention this because of our tendency to fall into one or the other extreme —for instance, an overstructuring of life and world followed by the reaction of understructuring; underwork as a reaction to overwork; protectiveness as a reaction to progressiveness . . . and so on.

Extremist postures abound: conservative/liberal, scientific/spiritual; arrogant/gentle; assertive/self-effacing. Single persons, fortunate to detect in themselves these extremist temptations, try always to see both sides of the picture and not to close any door to truth in the current and future circumstances with which they must deal.

This is not to imply that such persons are "fence sitters," incapable of taking a stand on any issue. To be an adult implies commitment. It is simply to specify as a mark of singleness this capacity for openness to all sides of a situation versus rigid fixation on one perspective. Inherent in this plea for openness is a warning regarding the ease with which a single person can fall into closed patterns of behavior and prejudiced opinions. I'll never forget the hard lesson I learned in this regard during my first entrance to the working world, the summer of my sixteenth year. I got a job in a toy manufacturing company in the order department. My immediate supervisor was a single middle-aged woman who made it clear from the first day that there was only one way to do these orders correctly and that was her way. It was sad to see how the other girls made fun of her as soon as she left the office. She had no friends in that company, yet she had worked there for years. Throughout that entire summer she never bent one inch in her routine. She was inflexible in her insistence on exact routinization. All initiative was promptly discouraged. To look at her face was to behold a mask of bitterness. She hardly ever smiled. Mostly she complained that others were too stupid to see things her way.

By contrast, what a delight it is to meet a warm, open, joyous single person who gently helps us to correct our one-sided course of thought, decision or action. This was Professor Andrew. The students gravitated toward his office whenever the pressures of exams and due papers became too much to bear. He always had coffee and cookies and a soft-cushioned chair into which we would sink to talk things over. Mainly he listened to the same litany of complaints voiced by the chorus of undergraduates who passed through his office over the years. He made each of us feel as if we were telling our woes for the first time. He had the understanding and patience to lift us out of our fixation on one part of the picture—for instance, "this miserable text"—so that we could see again the whole purpose of our study. The memory of his witness to the joy of being single and a servant to many remains with all of his students today.

The single person cares for others also by developing a critical consciousness. Practicing the art and discipline of meditative reflection, it becomes second nature, as it were, to critique gently but firmly situations in life that in any way fail to respect human rights and dignity. Because single persons of necessity value the singularity of every human being, they are critical of attempts to level originality or to reduce people's unique talents or gifts to the lowest common denominator.

This critical consciousness encompasses not only occasions where admonishment is called for, either of individuals or institutions; it also enables the single person to admire others and praise their worthwhile accomplishments. It helps enormously if singles take a foundational approach to human formation, since this approach is rooted in experience as such and takes its starting point from daily practice, not merely from specialized, theoretical principles. A merely ideological posture may cause us to admonish only those who disagree with us and to admire only those who support our position, instead of taking each stance at face value and seeing how it can be an articulation of something more foundational.

Critical consciousness demands that single persons also foster a sound intellectual life by selecting and reading good classical and contemporary literature that not only imparts information but also forms heart, mind and will. Such reading helps us to be attentive to and supportive of efforts to liberate fellow humans from injustice, from lack of mercy, compassion and peace. We are thus enabled to take a committed stand to uphold perennial human values whenever they are in danger of being violated. This stance would include a critique of any authority that denies human freedoms or any custom so encrusted by time that it ceases to answer real needs. What form this critique takes is dependent on the person's foundational calling and societal position. Singles do have the advantage, however, of operating in controversial circles without unjust offense to a family or community that may hold other views.

It follows that singles must be willing to bear responsibility for actions taken. That is why decision should be preceded by much reflection, prayer, appraisal and a realistic anticipation of the consequences. Sometimes it is better to remain silent than to speak, to consider the long run versus the short run, to witness to values more by living them hiddenly than by promoting them publicly.

All in all, single persons are aware of how important it is to be engaged in tasks that are meaningful, not popularly trivial. They realize that the business of living is serious and, in the light of the swift passage of time, inevitably dramatic. One must be a good, even an excellent, player on the stage of life. What is the use of remaining mediocre? of pursuing petty politics rooted in envy of excellence? of spending one's precious time in idle enterprises that corrode the spirit and make one a hapless victim of consumerism and passing cultural fads?

The single person must try to rise above these demeaning practices and treat each day with the seriousness it deserves— for each day is part of the fabric of formation that draws mankind toward the fullness of peace and joy. To treat life seriously is not to lose lightheartedness. It is essential to maintain one's sense of humor, to admit humbly that human freedom is always limited, that in any given situation one can only accomplish so much, and—God knows—that is never perfect. That is why we leave the rest up to Him.

Humor connotes an acceptance of life's limits, a benevolent appreciation of efforts full of eagerness yet always imperfect. It is good to propose the kind of world one would like to live in, while blessing things as they are and working from there. In *The Imitation of Christ*, Thomas à Kempis says it so well: "Man proposes but God disposes."

This fact does not diminish our esteem of human efforts to control the future. It simply kills unrealistic expectations that our way should prevail. Life may have other plans and we had better be prepared humorously to accept them. In these and many more ways, the single person develops a critical consciousness, sparked by the commitment to care for others as one cares for self and is cared for by God.

THE SPECIAL CARE OF SINGLE PARENTING

Couples who divorce, legally separate, or lose their spouse may find themselves thrust into the circumstance of single parenting. Caring for their children is now the responsibility not primarily of mother *and* father, but of mother *or* father. One must cope with the hard facts of economic support, custody rights, or visiting privileges, to say nothing of the inner pain of feeling betrayed, lonely, or full of grief. These facts force the single parent into a new formation situation. While dealing with personal hurts, one must also face with one's children the harsh reality of parental separation.

Many researchers note the anxiety and guilt children feel when such a loss occurs. Their parents may seek counseling at this time or simply grope for answers on their own. With or without professional help, parents suffer through this experience. They cannot pretend to their children that everything is fine. It takes openness, honesty and plenty of time to move from couple-oriented care to single parenting.

Children need not only physical but also emotional and spiritual care. Single parents have to help their children adapt to the demands of this new situation. Because mother has to work, she cannot be at home as much as her child would like. The time they do spend together has to make up in quality for what it lacks in quantity.

A single parent I know had primary responsibility for his children throughout their adolescent years. His work schedule and their school days coincided well, so weekends became immensely important. Saturdays and Sundays were family days. This decision left room for personal activities while assuring their togetherness at the dinner table and their sharing of house and garden chores. The best times were when they relaxed, sat around and talked. He believed in expressing his care for two daughters and a son through a willingness to listen to their problems and to offer any help he could. In due time, their life more or less returned to normal. By the time the children left for college, he had become, as he put it, "quite the expert in single parenting." Having accepted the challenge of this new circumstance, he found that it not only drew him closer to his children, but it left him needed extra time for recreation and reflection.

There are, of course, many different levels of single parental responsibility, depending on financial arrangements, on the ages and number of children, on the surrounding support of family members, and so forth. Behind these differences, one finds the common condition of singleness. What pertains to the spiritual formation of any single person applies to parents as well—with a few special considerations.

Single parents may experience more intense problems with loneliness. They may try to resolve these by becoming overly dependent on their children. This attempt is admittedly understandable, but it fails to respect sufficiently the child's need to be a child. It makes him or her a substitute spouse or adult friend. What started out as a solution to loneliness only leads to more confusion.

Single parents may not need to rely so heavily on their

children for solace if they feel understood and accepted by family members like their own parents or their brothers and sisters, as well as by their friends and other support groups like those begun in some churches for single parents. If such care is shown to them, they can widen the circle of care they want to extend to their children. This extended family of relatives and friends offers single parents and their children more room to grow in an atmosphere of mutual care and concern.

Single parents ought to seek ways of meeting one another and talking over their concerns for child care, their feelings of discouragement, and their newly found joys. Some see only the dark side of what has occurred, but, as in any crisis, so too in the case of single parenting, there is danger: What will happen to me and the children? There is risk: Did I make the right decision? And there is opportunity: How can I face this challenge courageously and become a better person through it?

Becoming a single parent may be a matter of circumstance due to widowhood, separation, or divorce, but it may also be a matter of choice. Increasingly, single adults are reaching out to care for homeless, handicapped or otherwise hard-to-place children. Thus it is appropriate in this discussion of singles as caring persons to mention the call some feel to become adoptive or foster parents as well as regular volunteers in programs like Big Brothers and Big Sisters. These kinds of commitments to children are not possible for all singles due to their assumed professional, charitable or prior family obligations. But there are a number of singles who may find such parenting as fulfilling for them as it is sustaining for a child in need of love and steady support.

Not being a single parent myself, I can only address the spiritual horizon out of which such a commitment should ideally emerge. This commitment to a child involves a pledge of lasting fidelity, hope and love. Single parents become the deepest influence on their child's initial formation. Case records show that these adoptive or homeless children are often deeply wounded in spirit if not in body. They need much nurturing love and affirmation to find themselves and to grow confident in their gifts and talents.

I have one friend who is a single mother of two children of biracial background. She herself grew up in a large family and always had an innate love for children, having cared for her younger brothers and sisters after her mother died. When she was of marriageable age, it was not possible for her to leave her family. After a while she was able to be at peace with her singleness and regard it as a true vocation. Looking back on those years from the perspective of her being a single parent, she sees that God did have a plan for her life. She would never have known these children, who mean so much to her, who need her love, had she married and raised her own family. Hearing her speak of her formation journey always increases my own faith in God's providential design for each of our lives.

She has been a single mother for several years. Her children were adopted, respectively, at age fourteen and eighteen months of age, a girl and a boy, both of whom are going into their teens. I asked her to write and tell me what she regards as the essential ingredient of the call within the call to singleness to become a single parent. What are the "musts" one must take into account if he or she wants to become a single father or mother able to handle this responsibility financially, physically, psychologically and spiritually? In her letter she replied:

> Loving children no matter what their condition has to be the basis of this commitment. And, if one does adopt, the commitment has to be to this person or to these persons for life. I think it's good to have had the experience of seeing brothers and sisters grow to maturity and perhaps helping them out. This makes one more realistic about the work and pain involved in child-rearing.
>
> By far the joys outweigh the pain, but it's the hard times one remembers most—their bouts with serious

illness, their having to face a discriminatory situation at school, their longing that never quite dies, to know something about their real parents. The demands made upon one to give them a sense of faith in themselves, to assure them that they have a future to look forward to, and above all, to give them unconditional love—these demands test the patience of all parents and of single parents in particular because they cannot be shared with a spouse.

There are many nights when I'd like to discuss the children's lives with an understanding father, but I have to make many crucial decisions alone. What I'm trying to say is: one has to be strong emotionally to bear this kind of responsibility and, speaking for myself, one has to have a firm faith in God and the conviction that He will see one through apparently insurmountable difficulties. This faith and the consequent actions it sustains present children with an in-depth experience of the Christian presence to life that should last.

If one is not up to the commitment implied in adoption but still has time, love and energy to spare, then I'd recommend foster parenting. In some cases this does lead to adoption but the requirements are different. Adopting children is a commitment to continuity. Their life continues through us and our life through them. Foster parenting is discontinuous but wonderful in its own right because it gives children a safe place to be for a while until they find themselves. But if the child becomes too problematic, the relation can be terminated and more expert help sought.

In both cases I would stress the importance of flexibility and openness. It is not only my children who grow and change, but I myself grow and change with them. I know that one of these days I'll have to let go of them and encourage their independence. This is a time I anticipate with mixed feel-

ings. On the one hand, I relish the thought that they have become strong enough under my care to lead responsible lives of their own while knowing where to go for assistance when needed.

On the other hand, I don't honestly anticipate having to cope all over again with loneliness. Though I did not adopt them to escape singleness, as some may unwisely do, I must admit that their presence does fill my life. It offers me the kind of community feeling a single person in the world does not know.

Single parents really aren't single in the strict sense. I must admit that their adopting children may have something to do with their not really wanting to be that solitary. Still I was alone before becoming a parent, and I hope that when the time comes I'll be able to face their departure gracefully. Don't let me exaggerate the issue either. There's always the chance I'll be a grandmother!

I feel much admiration for her thoughtful approach to parenting, and seeing her children convinces me that God has made a good match. She is there to help them resolve the usual problems of growing up, but I would venture to say that because of her singleness she is able to bring them a special gift too. She really celebrates their uniqueness and encourages them in every way to develop their God-given talents. She has taught them to live by Gospel values, to care for others as she has cared for them. In her family there is peace and a glimpse of the promise of what life is meant to be in the kingdom.

Suggested Readings

Edelwich, Jerry. *Burn-Out: Stages of Disillusionment in the Helping Professions*. New York: Human Sciences Press, 1980.
This seminal work portrays the four stages of disillusionment— enthusiasm, stagnation, frustration and apathy—that constitute

the "burn-out syndrome" in the human services. The work, based on extensive interviews with social workers, teachers, psychologists and other professionals, explores the causes of burn-out. Constructive intervention methods are proposed to assist individuals and institutions in recognizing and learning to live with each stage.

Huizinga, Johan. *Homo Ludens: A Study of the Play Element in Culture.* Boston: The Beacon Press, 1950.

The subject of play is approached not scientifically but historically. The author integrates the concept of play into that of culture. Play is not merely one among many manifestations of culture, but culture itself bears the character of play. Civilization arises and unfolds in and as play, and "Man the Player" ("Homo Ludens") deserves a place in our vocabulary.

Lee, Harper. *To Kill a Mockingbird.* New York: J. B. Lippincott, 1960.

This 1960 novel has since become an American classic. Set in Maycomb County, Alabama, the story is one woman's recollection of her upbringing in a small southern town. Its plot and significance revolve around "Scout's" father's principled views on human integrity as he attempts, as a single parent and the town lawyer, to raise his son and daughter in the midst of racial conflicts and tensions. A winning novel, it adds much dignity and hope to the parental role.

Mayeroff, Milton. *On Caring.* New York: Harper & Row, Publishers, 1971.

The reader is led through an analysis of the major ingredients of caring—such as patience, honesty, trust and humility—as well as some illuminating aspects of caring and the main characteristics of a life ordered through caring. A small text, it can be read easily by any parent, teacher, therapist, artist, civil servant or administrator interested in becoming a more caring presence for another person or for an entrusted task. Not through dominating or explaining, but through caring and being cared for, can one be said to be at home in the world.

Oates, Wayne E. *Confessions of a Workaholic.* New York: Abingdon Press, 1971.

In a lively style the author recounts his own addiction to work and how he has reformed. After discussing the origin of workaholism in social, religious and emotional influences, he identifies prevalent symptoms prior to addiction and offers practical suggestions for placing work in a new, more satisfying, and fulfilling perspective. The message of this book is the necessity of changing a pattern of life which consumes far more than it produces in those who are trapped in it.

O'Donoghue, Noel Dermot. *Heaven in Ordinarie: Some Radical Considerations.* Springfield, Ill.: Templegate, 1979.

In seventeen probing essays, O'Donoghue discusses themes that are relevant to every thoughtful Christian: "Vocation," "Horizons of Pathos," "Loneliness," "Belonging," "Playfulness," "The Dynamism of Tradition," "Creation and Participation" and many more. The author approaches spiritual development and the religious dimension at a reflective level, with reason as a guiding light in pursuit of truth and human reality, offering a rare blend in spiritual literature of simplicity, freedom and depth.

Thomas à Kempis. *The Imitation of Christ.* Ed. Harold C. Gardiner. Garden City, N.Y.: Doubleday, Image Books, 1955.

Written by a monk for monks, yet a springboard for all Christians concerned with the interior life, *The Imitation* is a series of meditations pointing the way by which all may follow the teachings and example of Christ's life. It is a timeless message of humble inspiration for all who seek the peace and confidence only God can offer.

van Kaam, Adrian. "Provisional Glossary of the Terminology of the Science of Foundational Formation." *Studies in Formative Spirituality,* II, 3 (November 1981), pp. 499–540.

The author distinguishes between uniqueness and individuality and presents terminology dealing with the hierarchy of life dimensions; the pride form; acceptance of limits; security directives; and practical appraisal.

7

****
****

Singles
as Cared for by God,
Singles at Prayer

In this discussion of care, we cannot overlook one key factor: the belief and lived awareness that each of us is cared for by God. Here we address what for me personally is an essential constituent of singleness, namely, one's relationship to the Sacred, to God.

In and with Him we are never alone in an ultimate sense. There is always Another to whom we can turn. This turning to Him does not mean a turning away from the world to pursue an otherworldy peace that smiles compassionately upon the plight of human suffering but does nothing about it.

Our turn to God is not an escape from reality but a way to go more deeply into it. We want to go to the wellspring from which all life and being emerges. We want to meet this Forming Mystery from whence all creation proceeds. This meeting occurs in some way whenever we behold the Timeless in time, the Infinite in the finite. Everywhere we see manifestations of the Divine Formation Mystery, even if we can never pierce its essence.

To speak of the single life as formative of a deep spirituality is to posit an ever-intensifying experience of faith, hope and love. We must have the faith that our life is part of God's providential plan for our personal salvation and the salvation of mankind as a whole. This faith makes possible our final commitment to the single life as a vocation, that is, as a calling from God and not merely a question of circumstances or cultural conditioning. We believe we have been called to singleness because this is the best way we can fulfill God's providential plan for our lives.

This act of faith increases our hope that God will not leave us orphaned (Jn. 14:18). He is with us now and shall be with us in eternity. To live in hope is to affirm the promise of ongoing intimacy with a loving God. Because He loves us, because He has loved us first (1 Jn. 4:10) we can reach out in loving presence, in patience and compassion to others. We are not afraid to love them with the same love by which God loves us—a love full of hope that lets the other be while fostering his or her best good.

Faith, hope and self-giving love are essential to the single life. Only to the degree that we acknowledge our being cared for by God can we experience each other as *Thou* and never as *It*. For this reason many single persons realize that casual, self-indulging sexuality can never make one happy. To treat the other as an object of genital gratification leaves one feeling harsh, empty and sadly unfulfilled. Real love can best be experienced between single persons when they reverence one another's integrity in God. Then they treat each other gently, with courtesy. They seek gracious ways of sharing their deepest feelings, for instance, in the intimacy of a trusting conversation. Physical affection is expressed within the boundaries of their mutual commitment to a life of *inclusive* vs. *exclusive* love. Again, because they sense how much they are cared for by God, they want to care for one another in the light of His love. Such love is more inclined to give than to take, to be for the other even at the risk of not receiving like love in return.

Single lovers discipline themselves to see timeless qualities of human likeness to God even in the most limited persons. Because they are not looking for "that one special someone," they see all people as special in God's eyes. Because they strive to live in a transcendent perspective, their love extends beyond the particular limits of a person to an appreciation of him or her as an expression of Divine Care.

In the next chapter, we will speak in more detail about friendship in the single life, but let us dwell here—in reference to the felt sense of being cared for by God—on the importance of prayer in the life of a single person.

I'd like to relate the prayer of singlehood first of all to what the poet John Keats has called "negative capability." By this he meant that attitude of mind that prevails when a person is capable of being in uncertainties, mysteries and doubts, without any irritable reaching after fact and reason. In other words, rather than seeking to come to premature closure about life, one lives in the mystery of knowing and not knowing. This openness to the Unseen yet Real constitutes true prayer. It is close to what Evelyn Underhill calls "practical mysticism" or that capacity to intuit the Invisible in the Visible, to sense a Presence beyond what one can grasp logically and to rest in Its benevolence.

At the center of each Christian's prayer life is the revelation that God has first loved us. He called us into being and formed us in His image and likeness. From the first instant of conception He is inviting us to be a unique member of His family and to give to the world some share of His own love. In Baptism all dimensions of our life are elevated by grace to participate through Christ in the eternal Formation Mystery that forms everything initially and keeps on forming us as whole graced persons.

To be a person means to be spirit, that is, to let the transcendent presence that I am sound through my humanness. For as human we are more than our vital impulses and functional ambitions. We are openness to Mystery. Our entire life is a dynamic searching for this More Than. A birth process is going on at all times as we move from one current life form to the next. In short, we change, we grow, we move on. This inner growth should keep pace with aging and outer activity.

Of primary importance to inner growth, and hence to the single person who must develop an interior life to survive, is prayer.

LIVING PRAYERFULLY

We must understand prayer in the widest possible sense. To say prayers is one thing, whereas to live prayerfully involves a lifetime of growing, as did the Lord, in age and grace and goodness before the Father (Lk. 2:52). How does this inner unfolding, so essential for wholesome single living, take place? It can only occur when we are in tune with the inspiration and action of the Holy Spirit in our human spirit. This means being open to divine directives in the midst of daily life. Do we pay attention to the subtle movements of the Spirit in our ordinary lives? These directives are seldom overwhelming. Most often they are quiet whispers (invitations, challenges, appeals) to respond in a more Christlike way to other people, to events and things.

To live prayerfully necessitates that we seek to uncover the deeper meaning of life. To do so implies that we live reflectively, in a meditative way, rather than compulsively, in a superficial manner that hungers after every passing fad. As transcendent selves, we aspire to go beyond what statistics can measure and to open ourselves to the depth dimension of reality, even though this option entails suffering. Did not the prayer life of Christ lead to the cross?

Prayerful living changes our attitude toward functional management and control. Prayer as a lived disposition even enhances efficiency. What alters is our sense of placing talents at the service of higher aspirations and inspirations to serve the kingdom of God. We want to use our gifts for His sake. We want to channel our ambitions toward the service of others. Paradoxically, we become even better at our task when we cease acting as if we have control over everything and give the controls over to God.

Spiritual formation is similarly enhanced when we respect the physical limits of our body and try not to push beyond them. We believe that peace of mind and body occurs when we obey the pace of grace in our lives. Since each person's energy level is different, prayerful living implies being in touch with one's body. As embodied spirits, we are mindful that a healthy organism is more conducive to meditation than an abused body. Single persons must guard against two aberrations in this regard: under- and overindulgence.

Underindulgence means that we disregard commonsense rules about nutrition, exercise, rest—choosing to eat on the run, compete fiercely on the court and snatch a few winks. We treat our bodies as if they do not count at all and wonder why it was so hard to pray. The answer is not to go on mortification binges where we fast ferociously and bend our brows in a sudden spurt of Bible reading. We must simply begin eating well-balanced meals, exercising wisely and getting enough rest.

Overindulgence is just as bad. Some of us are wont to pamper our bodies inordinately. We spend too much time seeking gourmet delights, following the cults of body-beautiful and refusing to take on any extra tasks that hamper our leisure and rest periods. In this case the body becomes an idol that in the end—because of its sensual demands—gives us no peace.

The answer again is to respect our vital organism without succumbing to unreflective impulses and unwise indulgences. We need to respond to others in an affectionate way while restraining our emotions. If we then place our physical and emotional energy at the service of God, He will use us to coform the kingdom, just as finely tuned instruments flowing together form a symphony. Perhaps prayerful living is best compared to such a symphony, each player freely creating sound through tuned instruments drawn together in orchestral formation by the conductor. How this sound pleases the ear and uplifts the spirit!

PRAYERFUL ABIDING WITH A TEXT

Prayer is thus a way to live as a unique, unified person in presence to the Divine Presence. One way to enter into His presence is to take a single text from the scriptures or another inspiring text and enter into the meaning of the words in the light of our life experience. Here is an example from my own experience of what happens in the single textual prayer of presence.

The text is: *Only in God be at rest, my soul* (Ps. 62:6).[1] I reflect: This rest is the embrace of love and the sigh of surrender. (The occasion of reflection is a few days prior to my hospitalization for major surgery that will mean a movement from one current form of life to another—in this case, due to the nature of the surgery, from the possibility of physical mothering to a confirmation of my vocation to singleness as a means of spiritual parenting.)

The reflection continues: at rest means to hover between silence and speaking, contemplation and action. This is truly an in-between time in my life. One part of it is ending; a new phase is beginning. Pain will mark its passing, but with God's help, my soul, my whole life, will gain a new start. Biological mothering ends; spiritual generativity renews itself and deepens the sense of my single vocation. No one but Jesus can be the Lord of my life. Only in His gentle caress can my soul find rest. This rest shall be my goal and His gift before, during and after the surgery.

A few days later, my reflection continued: I want to feel with His support the full weight of the limits and sadness of life so that, by facing this reality, I can also taste the deepest joy—the joy only acceptance of the cross can grant. Truly, only in the shadow of His cross can my soul rejoice.

The same text was in my mind and heart the evening be-

---

[1] "Rest in God alone, my soul!" is the *Jerusalem Bible* translation of Psalm 62:5.

fore surgery, when I wrote in my journal: I go into this ordeal
embraced by the love of family and friends and feeling the
total support of the Lord. A dear friend wrote this note to me
today: "May Our Lord grant you purity of heart at the center
of your being, so that you can see God in the gift of suffering
and repeat wholeheartedly, 'Only in God be at rest, my soul.'"

The text gathered around itself the trust I placed in God
and so I wrote to Him: In recent days I have felt strongly
that tug between ends and beginnings. You know, Lord, that
I see this ending of physical parenting for me as a symbolic
affirmation of your plan for my life as being one who nurtures
spiritually. I accept the surgery as a sign of my being chosen
from the beginning for the single life, sustained by the
generative tasks of teaching and writing. So I can say now
these words of Psalm 62 and mean them with all my heart.

Only in God. You alone are the Love of loves in my life.
I sense deeply your allness in my singleness.

Be at rest. Even from a biological perspective, this is the
most ideal state possible for healing. Help me to relax into the
surgery, to accept the pain, to cooperate with the medica-
tions, to fight nothing, to rest within the spiritual forces that
urge the body toward healing in good time. Help me to be in
a state of inner restfulness despite the trauma of organ re-
moval.

My soul. This is the inner person you love and call into
service despite human weakness. Sustain this life principle
that animates all my bodily functions. Be in me, Lord, as I am
in you. Lead me through this dark tunnel with trust and courage. Guide the hands of the surgeon and bring me into the
next phase of my life.

This prayer of trustful presence, emerging from abiding
in a sacred text, may not feel like much on the vital level. It is
not meant to produce a spiritual high. It arises from that silence in which the heart hears the Lord's voice telling us of
His love and assuring us that we need not be afraid. We
know in the midst of doubt and suffering there is Someone
upon whom we can rely. We resonate with the conviction that

no matter what happens we cannot stop God from loving us. We may forget Him, but He never forgets us. Each moment He calls us into being by that forming love that manifests itself not in fiery displays but in the ordinariness of every day.

We would like bells to clang, but we have to face instead drab routine. At times, when the sense of His absence is almost unbearable, He comes. He is there in those unexpected moments when we feel held and sustained in our singleness. He communicates with us in silence and solitude in such a way that we are opened in the depths of our being to His presence.

Because we are made in the image and form of God, we must find ways of integrating that mystery with our day-to-day social world and our immediate situation as teacher, nurse, secretary, sales clerk, poet, doctor, lawyer, laborer. The prayer of textual abiding welcomes God into every corner of our daily life. It creates dispositions that open us to the sacred ground of reality from whence emerges our personal formation history.

Sometimes I feel as if this text from the Book of Wisdom was written personally for me as a single woman:

> *When peaceful silence lay over all,*
> *and night had run the half of her swift course,*
> *down from the heavens, from the royal throne, leaped*
> *your all-powerful Word;*
> *into the heart of a doomed land the stern warrior*
> *leaped.*

> (Ws. 18:14–15)

I am often like that doomed land. I feel at times fed up with myself. Have I missed my calling by not being married? Have I been cheated by not enjoying the reciprocal union of marital, procreative love? Can I live with the empty space of those children I'll never have? At such moments I feel so unloved, so deserted, so dry. Then into my memory drifts a text like this one to redeem the desolation and discouragement. For into the doomed land of my life the all-powerful Word bounds. To this land of weakness, frailty and doubt He brings the balm of peaceful stillness. He reminds me that there are no answers, no easy solutions to the mystery of a person's life, to the inexorable decree of destiny. There are no techniques to dissolve spiritual darkness, no magic formulas to make the wounds better. There is only faith. There is only the peaceful stillness of the night, of the silence that encompasses everything.

Through the grace of textual abiding, I begin to experience the doomed land of human limits and uncertainty as mysteriously placed within the silent, forming plan of God. In Him my life takes on new purpose and meaning. It becomes an expression of that loving formation that pervades the universe and history. The little house of my life belongs within the lasting House of God, and in His House there is much light.

Such moments of contemplative dwelling take us out of the whirlwind of worldly consumption and production. They create a quiet space in our single lives. They restore the spiritual foundation we tend to forget. Once restored and cultivated, the fruits of this prayer flow over into our cultural participation. This practice in the life of a Christian can lead to renewed awareness of the Trinitarian Formation Mystery permeating humanity and world. In a secondary way this practice can and does heighten the effectiveness and attractiveness of our service in the Lord.

This kind of prayer is, in partnership with other ways of prayer, particularly suited to the single life. Let us turn to these now, beginning with prayers of petition or intercession.

INTERCESSORY PRAYER

Intercessory prayer, or prayer of petition, is a frequent part of my single life, especially when I bring before the

Lord, in addition to my needs, those of family members, friends, colleagues and students. In prayers of intercession we unite our will to God's and in faith and trust ask humbly for all that we need. This prayer is impossible without faith, for it begins where reason and natural means to accomplish human ends cease to be effective.

I sometimes call this my peasant prayer—a prayer God cannot refuse to answer in some way because it is uttered with no sophistication, only pure faith. I believe that if I ask, I shall receive; that if I seek, I shall find; that if I knock, the door shall be opened to me (Mt. 7:7-8). This prayer touches the heart of God because it is uttered in desperation. Like the Publican, we beseech God's mercy (Lk. 18:13). Like the Centurion's servant, we know that we are not worthy to receive the Lord, but that if He says so our soul, His servant, shall be healed (Lk. 7:6-7).

When all human means are exhausted, when we witness the futility of our own efforts, we turn to God for mercy, for healing, for the fulfillment of physical and spiritual needs. This prayer acknowledges what we singles often feel: that God alone can satisfy our heart's desire. It is when we are powerless, vulnerable and out of control that God can work most freely in our lives. We allow God to be God because we have been reduced to nothing. Sometimes this prayer is composed of only one word: Help! We pray full of confidence that God always responds to human desperation. He does not scorn the broken, humbled heart (Ps. 51:17).

Intercessory prayer is profoundly incarnational. It draws upon the formative powers of memory (all that He has done for us in the past); of imagination (all that He can do for His faithful); of anticipation (all that He shall do if we surrender wholly to Him). It is a prayer that places us on the razor's edge between God's incomprehensible mystery and mercy and our experience of His action in daily life. The way God manifests Himself is inclusive, meaning that it excludes nothing from the payment of a bill to the healing of an organism.

We can ask His help in anything small or great and somehow He'll be there.

It may come as no surprise to learn that at least one saint, Catherine of Siena, who was called by the Lord to live the single life, saw the connection between intercessory prayer and contemplation. Petition for her was a unitive way of prayer because it unites the soul with God in all things. It brings Him into every event of daily life and thus increases our experience of His presence. In her *Dialogue*, St. Catherine records the Father's invitation that we never relax our desire of asking for His help. Our intercessory prayers will serve as intermediaries between a sinful, forgetful world and a forgiving, merciful God. With every intercession we affirm the relationship of love between God and His people.

PRAYER AS CONVERSATION WITH GOD

Because single persons spend a lot of time alone, they usually resonate with the way of prayer recommended by St. Teresa of Avila, namely, conversation with Christ. In her own experience, she found it most consoling to keep up a running, interior conversation with her Divine Friend. This prayer brings with it a happy, childlike feeling of trust and companionship. We can talk to the Lord of our trials and small triumphs, of our failings and of our thanks for His forgiveness. We may find ourselves quite literally talking to Him while cooking supper or driving to work, before a class or after an important meeting. We soon learn that we can call upon Him at any moment and find Him near. At times this conversational intimacy may give way to moments of adoring distance or quiet nearness. Words fail to contain our gratitude and so we worship in silence.

In these conversations with Christ, we may find our thoughts and feelings falling more and more into line with His Word and Will. Maybe we began one of our talks full of misgivings about our capacity to take on some task. As we bring our litany of human weaknesses before Him, we soon find that they are not such insurmountable barriers after all. Enormous mountains to climb by ourselves alone become manageable foothills when He is beside us. We realize that without Him we can do nothing, but that with Him our insufficiency becomes a source of spiritual strength.

Conversations with the Lord thus cover a wide range of topics—as wide as the joys and sorrows of daily living. There is really nothing we do or have done that cannot be brought before Him. He understands it all. He illumines our minds when they are in darkness. He moves our wills despite indecision, touches our hearts and draws us toward loving action. In conversation we discover again and again that God is Father, Friend, Guide, Lover. He enjoys speaking with us as much as we enjoy talking to Him.

In these exchanges, verbal or wordless, each of us in our uniqueness experiences the personal love of God and grows toward new heights of transcendent presence. We gain courage to bear with misunderstanding, with the overt or subtle ridicule of those who do not understand or respect a single style of life. When anger or frustration seems to get the best of us and we have no one to talk to at that moment, we are never at a loss, for our Divine Friend is always ready to listen.

Humble, at times disobedient, doubtful and afraid, we turn to Him and tell all. It might happen that we shed a few tears in the telling. They become an expression of the repentant nature of certain conversations. On other occasions, our tears may express an overflow of gratitude and joy. God's goodness so overwhelms us that we weep with relief. A thousand thanks would not be enough. He has heard our prayers. He has given us all that we asked for, and much more.

These conversations may become so habitual that we find ourselves living continually in the presence of God. What could be a more delightful state than this for single persons? People think they are alone but they are really at-one with God. He is our strength and salvation—not fame or status or popularity. He is the Forming Mystery in whom we place our entire trust. He alone can grant the grace of inner transformation.

As we grow in the art of conversing with God, we realize that it is not enough to set aside special times of prayer and retreat. It is certainly not enough to give God the dregs of our day, the time left over after everything else is done. No, He wants us to live in conversational nearness, to pray without ceasing (1 Th. 5:17). Ceaseless prayer is not a matter of saying prayers but, again, of conversing with God as our most intimate Friend. Then we cannot help but live in His presence, either acknowledging our nearness verbally or in silent adoration.

For what is conversation but a frequent turning to Him whom our heart loves most? If the main aim of the Christian single life is not to make primary our love relation with God, then what is it? No one but the Lord can fulfill human longings, and these longings are felt acutely by single persons. Is it any wonder, then, that we are drawn to converse with Him?

FORMATIVE READING HELPS PRAYERFUL LIVING

Formative reading is an excellent aid to the life of prayer, since it gives us direct access to Holy Scripture and the writings of the masters of our formation tradition. While Christians in general ought to value this kind of reading, it seems to be essential for singles. To live a spiritual life does not happen automatically. It requires discipline, vigilance of heart, and an ongoing renewal of our good intentions. Mind, memory and imagination need to be nourished on the word of God revealed in the Scriptures and validated experientially in the literature of spirituality, both classical and contemporary. Formative reading facilitates that transformation of heart which makes the single person more like the Lord to whom we have given our lives. It puts us in touch with the wisdom of the Church while stirring our heart's longing for God.

What are the basic guidelines pertinent to developing this art and discipline? Briefly, when we have selected our text with the intention of reading it formatively, we can begin this exercise by placing ourselves in the presence of God and asking Him to bless us in this time of reverent attention to the word. Such reading forgoes any tendency toward speed and purposefully slows down. What matters now is not quantity (how much I read) but quality (the way in which I read). I am more interested in allowing my heart to be touched than in merely gathering more information.

In other words, to paraphrase a common Benedictine adage: In formative reading I subsume my love of learning to my desire for God. I cease trying to master the text and, so to speak, allow the text to master me. I become docile like a true disciple or one who is willing to be taught and to be led by words radiant with Christian truth.

As I read, I may choose to mark whatever in the text really touches me. Either at that moment or later, following the reading session, I try to dwell further upon what these words are saying to me. I may take a few moments between readings to lift my eyes from the text and to reflect upon it. As an aid to the reflective process, I may choose to write my thoughts out more fully in a formative reading notebook. In these reflections I begin to uncover the many ways in which God uses the text to move my heart away from selfish concerns and toward self-giving love. The information I necessarily receive from the text is thus applied to personally formative life situations. For instance, I perceive in this reading an opportunity to better understand my single commitment and much encouragement to live it fully.

When a feeling of resistance to the text occurs, it often means that I am being reminded—somewhat painfully—of an authentic formation ideal neglected or forgotten. God chooses this reading to call me back to Himself. He uses the vehicle of the text as a way of awakening repentance and placing me back on the path of fidelity to my vocation.

In case I come across passages that are time-bound in their symbolic or philosophical context, I simply let these go by and go on to find those timeless passages that convey the perennial wisdom of spiritual deepening. Such passages inevitably tap into the foundations of human and Christian formation. It is on the solid rock of these foundations that we strive to build our single vocation. Only then can we go forth confidently to share these treasures of the formation tradition with others in the world.

As a way of encouraging singles to engage in this practice, let me profile my own experience. Prior to reading the text I have chosen, I say a short prayer to the Holy Spirit with the intention of placing myself in the proper receptive mood. I then turn to the text as one turns to greet a good friend. Even the way I handle the book tells me how important it is not to be rushed, but reflective. I remind myself that now is the time to stand in one spot and go deeper, to dwell upon the text. I do not expect this reading to solve problems; I go to it hoping to imbibe any spiritual lights that may come in the course of the next half hour or so. Nothing may happen, but that is no reason to give up. It is advisable to read on silently or in a soft, slow voice, awaiting the moment God may address me through these words.

This reading guides me gently yet firmly into the truths and mysteries of my faith. The more I dwell on these texts (for instance, the *Confessions of Saint Augustine*, the poems and commentaries of St. John of the Cross, *The Imitation of Christ*), the more I see emerging from them new lights, fresh appeals, challenging paths to follow. When this happens, I know that the words of the text serve as a bridge to bind my life to the Divine Word. Over this bridge He communicates His way and truth to me. He uses the art and discipline of formative reading to enrich my single life, to refresh my solitary search for meaning, to assure that my interior life will not be depleted.

In formative reading the pressure to compete or to succeed is diffused. I have no task to finish, nothing demanding to accomplish. All that is required is that I relax and remain open to whatever insights the text may awaken. Five lines or five pages—what does it matter as long as I am present to what I read? Instead of aggressively manipulating the text to suit my needs, I simply let it speak. Thanks to this reverent, appreciative approach, real growth in spirituality can occur. Even so, backsliding does not cease. It seems as if every inch of growth in the spiritual life is preceded by miles of retreat. Still we trust that God understands our hesitation to make a total commitment and gives us the grace to try again.

Aridity may also occur when I do formative reading, but this is not a sign to give up. That is when discipline is most needed—when the honeymoon period of a spiritual practice is over and I am faced with the challenge of doing this kind of reading even when I do not feel inclined in that direction. I cannot force formative reading to bring me into the felt presence of the Lord. I can only ready myself for that gift of intimacy and rejoice when it comes. For the most part I must wait in a patient, listening posture. This much seems sure: that through formative reading the hidden life of grace does its work of transforming my soul. I am being led, whether I know it or not, to a deeper single life in and with the Lord. The most I can say after a while is that something happened inside and I said yes. Growth in singleness is, after all, a quiet thing. Over the years, by responding to the directives revealed in the texts of the formation tradition, I find the self God intends me to be. In this way, formative reading becomes a pathway to conversion and vocational commitment.

Though formative reading depends on our love for inspiring words, it teaches us the importance of silence as well. For, after a set time of reading, we come to a natural moment of fullness, as when we have enjoyed a good meal. It is time now to close the text and assimilate its teaching, to diminish input and think about how to apply what we have read to our here-and-now situation. What speaks to us at this moment when words fall silent? There may be no answer, only more silence. We have been well fed at the table of the Lord, so let us enjoy this sabbath moment.

United with God via the bridge of formative reading, we are more able to face the difficulties associated with living a single, spiritual life in today's world. Clearly, any style of life is limited. Our reading has shown us that no family, community, parish or profession is perfect. In fact, nothing on this earth is perfect. If we expect it to be, we shall end up living in illusion. Only when we face the limits of earthly existence and accept that without God we can do nothing, only in that moment of truth, are we living in the suffering and joy of singleness.

Suggested Readings

Bloom, Anthony. *Beginning to Pray*. New York: Paulist Press, 1970.
    A book for anyone who wishes to speak to God, based on talks given by the author to people who had never before prayed. We must simply enter into the realm of God and not seek information about it. The day when God is absent, when he is silent—that is the beginning of prayer.

Catherine of Siena. *The Dialogue*. Trans. Suzanne Noffke, O.P. New York: Paulist Press, 1980.
    This work, dictated by St. Catherine while in a state of ecstasy to her secretaries, is a unique example of "ecclesiastical" mysticism. It is a mystical exposition of the necessary integration of contemplation and action, the lived dynamic of knowledge and love, which is at the heart of God's saving hope for our lives.

Ellul, Jacques. *Prayer and Modern Man*. New York: The Seabury Press, 1970.
    Aware of the many difficulties facing persons who desire a life of prayer in a technological society, Ellul reviews the possibilities for undertaking such prayer today.

Lefevre, Perry D., ed. *The Prayers of Kierkegaard*. Chicago: The University of Chicago Press, 1956.

Over one hundred of the prayers of Kierkegaard are gathered in this volume from his published works and private prayers, illuminating not only his own life of prayer but also serving as a book of personal devotion for Christian readers today. Following this collection is a reinterpretation by the author of the life and thought of Kierkegaard, who is revealed as fundamentally a religious thinker. In this new perspective, the reader discovers Kierkegaard's inner sense of vocation and his lifelong concentration on the problem of becoming a Christian. Certain that Kierkegaard was primarily a religious thinker and that his central problem was that of becoming a Christian—of realizing personal existence—the editor/interpreter intends to take the reader to the religious center of Kierkegaard's existence. From this perspective faith is seen to be Kierkegaard's goal and prayer as the sole means of moving toward that goal. This thesis is elaborated by an examination of Kierkegaard's own piety and his thought on the place of prayer in the life of the Christian.

Merton, Thomas. *Contemplative Prayer*. New York: Doubleday, Image Books, 1971.

In Merton's words, this book is a practical nonacademic study of prayer—the fruit of several decades of reflection and experience. In his familiar, conversational style, the author illumines the hard realities and upheavals of authentic prayer as well as the joy, reverence and expectation that inform it. He is as present to the living traditions of prayer in the Church as he is to the spiritual inertia and lack of confidence that mark the contemporary Christian's disregard and fear of prayer.

Muto, Susan Annette. *Approaching the Sacred: An Introduction to Spiritual Reading*. Denville, N.J.: Dimension Books, 1973.

The art and discipline of spiritual reading is a means for creating an inner atmosphere of receptive attention to God's love and will in and through the writings of the spiritual masters. This text discusses common obstacles and facilitating conditions associated with this attempt to reclaim our longing for God's self-revelation here and now in our lives.

——. *Steps Along the Way: The Path of Spiritual Reading*. Denville, N.J.: Dimension Books, 1975.

A sequel to *Approaching the Sacred,* this text offers further insight into the art and discipline of spiritual reading as well as a lively and perceptive study of the ways men and women have struggled to find God in their daily lives, such as the way of unknowing; the way of imitation; the way of spiritual childhood; and the way of ceaseless prayer.

——. *The Journey Homeward: On the Road of Spiritual Reading.* Denville, N.J.: Dimension Books, 1977.

The final volume of three on the art and discipline of spiritual reading, this work focuses on the reading of spiritual texts as a journey toward God. Part One considers the attitudes necessary in the person searching for a home in God. Part Two looks at what happens on the journey itself. Drawing upon classical Christian spiritual texts, each chapter integrates the wisdom of the masters with everyday life experiences and concludes with a personal reflection and prayer on a text of St. John of the Cross.

——. *A Practical Guide to Spiritual Reading.* Denville, N.J.: Dimension Books, 1976.

This book fills a deeply felt need among serious Christians who are convinced that they should engage in regular meditative reading. It is a practical aid answering such common questions as: What do I read? How can I do so effectively? How do I distinguish between more and less essential readings? This is a unique guide for any and all who desire to develop a formative approach to spiritual reading.

Nouwen, Henri. *Reaching Out: The Three Movements of the Spiritual Life.* New York: Doubleday, 1975.

This book is written in the conviction that the quest for an authentic Christian spirituality is worth the effort and pain involved, since in the midst of this quest we can find signs offering hope, courage and confidence. The author sees our spiritual ascent occurring in three essential stages: the movement from loneliness to solitude (our relationship to ourselves); the movement from hostility to hospitality (our relationship to others); and the final, most important movement, from illusion to prayer (our relationship to God).

O'Connor, Elizabeth. *Eighth Day of Creation: Gifts and Creativity.* Waco, Tex.: Word Books, 1971.

This devotional book gives one spiritual exercises and scriptural meditations designed to enable one to discover his or her own spiritual gifts. It is an excellent book to use with a group or by oneself in connection with reading St. Paul's discussion of gifts in I Corinthians. Ms. O'Connor is the author of many other excellent books on prayer life and the inward journey, books that stress the importance of focusing on various appropriate scriptural passages.

Steere, Douglas V. *Dimensions of Prayer.* New York: Harper & Row, Publishers, 1963.

Out of a lifetime of experience as a Quaker philosopher and spiritual director, the author assures us that in learning to pray, no laboratory is needed but a room; no apparatus but ourselves. The Living God is the field of force into which we enter in prayer, and the only really fatal failure is to stop praying and not to begin again. Steere claims that "Stillness, waiting, and patience before the Lord are authentic dimensions of the human perceptive equipment. These dimensions have been scandalously undervalued and ignored in our time. They need to be reinstated and used with an intensity of dedication comparable to that found in the pursuits of scientific investigation." This book is written to encourage precisely such practice and dedication, believing that prayer is for the spiritual life what original research is for science.

Underhill, Evelyn. *Practical Mysticism.* New York: E. P. Dutton & Co., 1915.

In this classical introduction to the methods and practice of mysticism for those who have little or no prior knowledge of the subject, Underhill explains what mysticism is and what it has to offer the average person: how it can help to simplify one's life, increase personal efficiency in the world and harmonize the duties and ideals of one's active life. The author's other works on the mystical life include the established classic *Mysticism* and several shorter works which followed thereafter: *The Mystic Way, The Essentials of Mysticism* and *The Golden Sequence.*

van Kaam, Adrian; and Susan Muto. *Practicing the Prayer of Presence.* Denville, N.J.: Dimension Books, 1980.

An excellent text drawing upon classical spiritual literature which aims to deepen our awareness of God's presence in daily life and to bring us closer to God. The need for contemplative presence is discussed at length. Differences between secular meditation and Christian prayer of presence are drawn in a revealing way. An instructive consideration of obstacles to growth in prayerful presence and conditions for growth in presence to the Divine Presence helps the reader to practice the prayer of presence in his or her own life.

——. "Provisional Glossary of the Terminology of the Science of Foundational Formation." *Studies in Formative Spirituality,* III, 1 (February 1982).

These glossary terms develop the theory of formative social presence and describe social-presence erosion; formative social and personal justice; fantastic vs. realistic appraisal; and the social exaltation spiral.

8

****
****

Friendship
and the Single Life

The single person, like every human being, needs to experience the gift of warm, caring relationships. Since the option of marital union is not present, the outlet for such intimacy lies in true friendship, or what I prefer to call the quality of befriending. We cannot willfully force friendship, but, if we remain open, it usually comes as God's gift into the lives of single persons, who themselves know what it means to be a friend.

Such persons are trustworthy and trusted. They do not make arbitrary demands on other people, though they do feel comfortable asking for help when necessary. Then, too, they are available when their friends need them. They are open about their vocation and its consequent commitments. Their respect for originality creates a relaxing atmosphere, freed from tactics of seduction or manipulation. Above all, befriending leads to a quality of encounter that fosters personhood between partners while opening them to the Divine Person in whom they both originate.

Befriending is not a cut-and-dried enterprise, but an ever-present risk, challenging the friends to face honestly their strengths and weaknesses and to relate to one another in tenderness and trust, knowing that the Lord they both love stands patiently in forgiveness between them.

This faith is at the basis of every soul-friendship. Faith makes it possible for us to talk to one another and to God about our secret hopes and fears, our successes and failures. Together we can pray to Him to guide the decision-making process and any actions that follow. We trust that God will befriend us as we have befriended one another.

The solitude, so loved by single persons, enables them to be with others in compassion and companionship. This capacity can be traced to the respect for privacy etched into the single person's soul. The profound belief that each person is made in the image and form of God impels single persons to reverence this holy center of privacy, to do nothing to violate it. Others are cherished for their uniqueness before God.

Thus, to reiterate something I've found to be true in my own life, without conspicuously seeking this gift, single persons over the years are usually blessed with a fine set of friends, members of the same or opposite sex. Some of these friendships are deeper than others, lasting a lifetime. Often they are formed in the context of a shared profession where colleagues can offer one another a kind of support association.

In this light, sexual expression means much more than mere "sex," than doing or not doing "it." The single male and the single female, who live with the Lord as their center, witness to the wholeness of the masculine and of the feminine and to the way in which these two sides of being human complement one another.

Single persons are and must be warm, vivacious, fully alive. They are not demeaned by empty sexual experience but wholly in touch with what it means to be male or female. Because they respect each other's integrity as persons, they can seek the joy of companionship. To be a real friend means to treat the other always as a unique subject, not as an object of self-gratification. This kind of treatment is sustained by mutual presence to the Transcendent. Just as the Holy blesses us in our wholeness, so we are called to bless one another. Just

as He wills our total good, so must we will the entire good of
the friends He gives to us. By thus serving the best interests
of one another, single friends stand in the culture as reminders of the transcendent aspirations all persons experience, even if they are unable to voice them.

Let us look at the larger horizon against which singleness
and single friendships unfold. We tend to forget that before
one chooses any state of life in the world, he or she is single.
In fact, only to the degree that people accept the burden and
blessing of their uniqueness can they enjoy a happy, realistic
life as married couples or members of a conventual community. These vocations will always contain the single component, no matter how much togetherness they grant.

It is a misconception, therefore, to identify the single vocation mainly in relation to the marital life—as if singleness
had no identity of its own. Some still hold the false notion
that only through the inability to marry does one discern a
vocation to singleness. This "poor soul," though sad at heart
at being a "loser," resigns him- or herself to a single life and
then tries to live as meaningfully as possible, making a few
friends here and there but finding it terribly difficult to live
without an exclusive partner. Others hold the equally false
notion that singles have either refused or not found their call
to the religious life in a convent or monastery.

This line of reasoning places singleness below marriage
or conventual life, unfairly relegating it to a second-class position. Clearly, before anyone is married, vowed or ordained, he
or she is single. If a marriage ends due to separation or death
of a spouse, one is single again. Because singleness predates
marriage or community membership, it must not be defined
negatively in relation to them. We ought to celebrate this
state of life in its own right as giving joyful witness to the
uniqueness inherent in the human experience.

Still, it is difficult for some to acknowledge the beauty
and dignity of singleness as such. They may even go so far as
to regard being single as a kind of curse, an alienating condi-

tion resulting from the entrance of sin into the world when
humanity discovered its separateness from each other and
from God. To prove that singleness is one of the host of evils
in which all share, they refer to the Book of Genesis in which
God saw that it was not good for Adam to be alone and so
gave him a mate. However, Adam and Eve's God-given
togetherness was broken apart by sin, and the curse of
singleness became a horrible reality. Man was out of tune
with himself and God. The conclusion of this line of reasoning is that God never intended singleness, no more than He
intended war, famine, pain, disease or death. Man brings
these evils upon himself. The question becomes what to do if
one is cursed with the stigma of being single. How can one
bear such a burden?

All kinds of pious suggestions could be given, beginning
with the necessity of accepting this stigma as a call from God
to surrender idle expectations about being married and to
start to make the best of one's singleness by working hard and
making many friendships. Thus single living is something we
must struggle to overcome. It is not accepted as a gift in its
own right, as a distinct and honorable calling from God.

Does it not occur to us that God may have made Adam
alone and unique exactly to express the profound mystery of
our original, never-to-be-duplicated, human formation? He
first created one person in celebration of uniqueness; only
then did He give this person a mate in celebration of togetherness. Out of solitude came the quest for solidarity, and not
the other way around. Try as we may, we cannot reason our
way out of original aloneness. Uniqueness precedes union
once we leave our mother's womb. Even infants bear the
traits of a unique personality that adapts itself to the togetherness of a family unit. Ultimately, it is in our uniqueness that
we are united with God. What separates us from Him is not
singleness but sins rooted in the pride system. We could say
that singleness is the greatest gift He gives because it manifests the depth of His singular, celebrative love for each

unique creature (the human being above all) in His kingdom.

LOVING ONE ANOTHER EQUALLY

In light of God's love for us, single persons try to love
others in a nonpossessive, nonmanipulative, self-giving, compassionate way—and that is not easy. It takes a lifetime of
discipline and prayer, plus daily practice. The key to such
befriending is charity—a human attempt to love others with
the love with which we have been loved by God. This rule of
charity is beautifully expressed by St. John:

> *My dear people,*
> *let us love one another*
> *since love comes from God*
> *and everyone who loves is begotten by God and*
> *   knows God.*
> *Anyone who fails to love can never have known God,*
> *because God is love.*
>
> *God's love for us was revealed*
> *when God sent into the world his only Son*
> *so that we could have life through him;*
> *this is the love I mean:*
> *not our love for God,*
> *but God's love for us when he sent his Son*
> *to be the sacrifice that takes our sins away.*
> *My dear people,*
> *since God has loved us so much,*
> *we too should love one another.*
>
> *If anyone acknowledges that Jesus is the Son of God,*
> *God lives in him, and he in God.*
> *We ourselves have known and put our faith in*
> *God's love toward ourselves.*

God is love
and anyone who lives in love lives in God,
and God lives in him.

(1 *Jn.* 4:7–11, 15–16)

We may be helped in this endeavor to love charitably if we recall the teachings of St. Teresa of Avila and St. John of the Cross, who regard love as a matter of treating each other "equally." St. John specifically stresses the need for "equal love and equal forgetfulness" in his cautions to celibates. They are not to love one person more or less than another, for they will soon err. In accordance with the second part of the Great Commandment, the love of charity must be universal and equal whether we feel a spontaneous liking for the other or not. The command is to love equally, as God loves, not to confine affection to those few special friends He does send.

This counsel facilitates our call as singles to love inclusively as distinct from the exclusive love between spouses. Naturally, their love does not exclude others; it only excludes another man or woman as primary. If we love with equal love and equal forgetfulness, we will not betray our vocation to singleness by loving one person to the possible exclusion of others who may need our help and affection. Certain people will call forth our capacity to love more than others; they are the ones toward whom we feel a graced affinity. However, in keeping with our single life call, this affinity, no matter how deep, does not flow over into an exclusive, reciprocal marital union. In other words, as single persons the remembrance of our love for another must be combined with forgetfulness of exclusivity. Only then can we love others equally while surely loving some other persons more especially. What helps here is the recollection that as singles our first and exclusive love belongs to God and hence that we can and must love others with "equal love and equal forgetfulness."

What happens if we love "unequally"? A single friend told me of her experience with a married couple. For all kinds of reasons she began to feel more love and liking for the husband than for the wife. As this love, innocent as it was, began to show through, it aroused in his wife feelings of resentment, jealousy and envy. She felt excluded from the little secrets they shared due to a mutual work situation. Though on the surface his wife responded to their relationship with humor and at times encouraged their togetherness, she was clearly seething inside. What was called for in this case was a good dose of forgetfulness on my friend's part in regard to her emotional and professional attachment to the husband. She had to show genuine and equal interest in, as well as respect for, his wife. Such discipline is essential if we are to remain faithful to our single vocation.

Equal love, in the words of St. Paul (1 Co. 13:4–13), is always patient and kind; it is never jealous, boastful or conceited, rude or selfish. Love of this sort does not take offense; it is not resentful; it does not come to an end. In other words, Christ-centered love always respects the rights of others and fosters their good. To give a few concrete examples: Where there is strife, the single-hearted lover seeks avenues of reconciliation. When tempers flare and impatience prevails, someone has to be courageous enough to propose a cooling-off period. If people are too busy to be courteous or hospitable, singles try to compensate in some small way for this lack of respect.

Thus we are called to set high standards that exemplify the art of loving. This means rising above the tendency not to get involved with others and truly befriending them. Such loving includes the risk of falling into emotional exclusiveness and consequent envy and jealousy. It also includes the risk of betrayed trust, mutual strife and power struggles. But what is the alternative? A selfish, little life, isolated and withdrawn, that casts a shadow over the single vocation as such. Too often single persons end up without any friends because they fear the risk of loving. Here again, if we apply the caution of St. John of the Cross, we can open ourselves to the gift of lov-

ing friendship while maintaining the proper stance of detachment and decorum.

By the same token, we are able realistically to bear with
the faults of others and still go on loving them. Having faced
so radically their own fallibility, single persons can identify
compassionately with the wounded condition in which we all
live. The advice St. Teresa of Avila gives to her sisters in *The
Way of Perfection* might be applicable here. She simply tells
them to commend to God any sister who is at fault and to
strive on their own part to practice the virtue that is the opposite of the other's fault. By making determined efforts to do
this, one sister teaches the other by her deeds what she could
perhaps never learn by words, or gain by punishment.

Such discrete checks and balances contribute to the
befriending capacity of single persons and enable them to be
with others in a charitable way. To embrace Christ as the
center of one's life is to embrace everything and everyone in
Him. We see and appreciate all of creation as a manifestation
of His goodness and love. The distance and detachment characteristic of such affectionate, respectful loving enables others
to witness in single persons the transforming effect of a firm
commitment to Christ. To imitate Him is to attain the grace
of loving others as God has loved us.

LOVING FAMILY MEMBERS
WHILE LIVING SINGLY

Single persons must manifest the same kind of committed
and detached loving toward family members as they do toward friends. This quality of love is especially called for in
relation to one's parents. Notwithstanding their goodwill,
some parents may try to dominate the adult lives of their single children. It is hard to let go of them, to really let them
live their own life, when no wife or husband comes in between. Many a single person has unwisely and too early in
life forfeited his or her right to a congenial, compatible style

of formation out of a noble, but perhaps false, sense of obligation to widowed or aging parents.

Admittedly, some singles prefer to remain attached to their parents during their lifetime and find a great deal of altruistic fulfillment in this commitment. They may even develop a mature friendship with their parents, that is, one freed from false guilt feelings and respectful of privacy. Even in these cases singles have to be careful, especially in middle age, that a creeping resentment toward one or both parents does not emerge due to a gnawing awareness of the many opportunities offered by life that had to be missed because of this obligation—however joyfully one consents to it. Then, too, singles who have always lived at home may later in life be faced with the problem of working through their aloneness while managing all household details on their own. Singles who leave home cope with these problems at an earlier age, usually in their twenties.

Similarly, singles have to be careful of the ways in which they befriend other relatives, especially those closest to them, like brothers and sisters, nieces and nephews. The love between them should be genuine and joyful, but not overly demanding or interfering. Singles ought not to build upon these family relations to the exclusion of other friends and associates. One woman I know can never go to a university function or social gathering without taking her parents along. It is easy to slip into a pattern of "steady dates" with other family members, thereby building mutual-dependency relations. For instance, while singles may understandably delight in their status as "favorite" aunt or uncle, they try not to interfere unduly with the child's upbringing. With relatives as with friends, the rhythm of distance and nearness must be respected.

Another bit of advice from St. Teresa of Avila to her sisters comes to mind as relevant to singles. In *The Way of Perfection* she notes in no uncertain terms that inordinate attachment to relatives is the hardest thing for the sisters to rid themselves of when they enter the monastery. She can understand, therefore, why people flee from their own part of the country, if it helps them. By the same token, she does not believe that the answer to detachment is found by fleeing from any place in a physical sense. Detached yet committed loving is only attained by opening one's heart and soul to the all-inclusive love of Christ. Just as one finds everything in Him, so for His sake one must forget everything.

Common sense tells us the same thing. It is not always possible or feasible for single persons to leave their hometown or city. They may like the city or value being close to home. For some singles, mainly for financial reasons, it is not even feasible to leave their parents' home, much as they may want to establish their own residence. But it is possible and necessary to be and remain firmly single in one's heart and to make this commitment clear accordingly to family members.

For instance, a family member ought not to seek information concerning the whereabouts of an adult working single person on evenings and weekends unless this is freely offered. Neither should one screen mail or phone calls or invade the privacy of one's apartment or room uninvited. Singles have to make it perfectly clear to other relatives that they need and deserve their privacy; otherwise, they leave themselves wide open at thirty-four to be treated as if they were fourteen.

There are an infinite number of ways to convey the message to others that they must accept and respect the rights and privileges of the single vocation. For example, I have a device on my phone that enables me to silence the ring when I am too busy studying or writing to answer it. When family members ring and receive no answer, they assume I'm at home working or reading or entertaining friends, and they wait for me to call them.

The importance of accustoming relatives to the demands of singleness cannot be overstressed. In our eagerness to please people, or better still, in our fear of being unpopular and perhaps standing alone, we may allow ourselves to be treated as children and to respond as such. This treatment only demoralizes a single person and indirectly makes it difficult for the rest of us to be treated with the full respect our vocation deserves.

While setting these conditions of detached loving, we must never expect total cooperation. Despite out best efforts to grow up, patterns of childish behavior between parents and their little boy or girl persist. We must rise above these regressive patterns with humor and forgiveness. We are ultimately the losers if we cannot let go of our irritation. Like it or not, parents and relatives do interfere with our best laid plans. Hence these can never be so rigid as to exclude needed compassion and flexibility. After all, mothers and fathers, brothers and sisters, aunts and uncles, nieces and nephews generally act out of goodwill and deserve the benefit of the doubt. It also remains true that no matter how old we are, there are times when mother really does know best!

Returning for a moment to the virtue of flexibility, we find it indispensable for singles. Our vocation grants us the freedom to be flexible. While our lives reflect a definite direction, we must be open to the grace of the moment, ready to give up futile attempts to control life so that we can flow with the gifts and challenges of every new day. It helps if we try continually to take a wider view of things, a more transcendent perspective that enables us to trust in a Power greater than ourselves and our necessarily limited vision. Only in surrender to God's will, written in the directives of our daily situation, can we become peaceful, reconciling persons in the family and community God calls us to serve.

Conflicts will arise that can pose a danger to compassion and peace, but they may offer us as well an opportunity to face what is wrong and to work toward a more respectful relationship. The worst thing that can happen between family members is for old angers to fester until they become gaping wounds, precluding peaceful reconciliation.

As good friends and open families know, conflicts and crises are occasions for growth. Constructive, not destructive, arguments clear the air and often lead to a reaffirmation of love, trust and mutual commitment. They compel us to reflect on the past, present and future formation of our relationship. Through formative crises and the pain they evoke, we can grow more compassionate toward one another, learning in the process how to be more responsive to genuine requests for understanding and help. It is most often in times of crisis that we discover our shared vulnerability and our need to care for one another as God has cared for us.

BEFRIENDING AS A RESOLUTION OF LONELINESS

Two types of loneliness pertain to the quality of befriending, these being primary and secondary. Primary loneliness entails the loss of a faith-friendship with God. Whether we feel His presence or His absence, we must not lose faith and trust in His friendship. Such a loss does not happen all at once. It is due usually to the process of erosion of our prayer life, combined with the pursuit of worldly goals as ultimate. This slow but steady neglect of the spiritual life catches up with single persons, who sooner or later feel emptied out by the demands and disappointments of superficial, self-indulgent living. They complain of a pervasive sense of loneliness, often accompanied by depression and near despair.

Loss of friendship with God severs them from the only lasting source of comfort there is for single persons. By contrast, befriending God in faith, as we are befriended by Him, readies us for being filled with the joy of His presence and encourages us to remain faithful, though we may be experiencing His absence. Only if we forfeit this bond to God does living alone lead to primary loneliness.

It follows that secondary loneliness is due to withdrawal from our neighbors, associates, friends and family. Some singles shy away from any kind of intimate encounter. They wear their solitude like a bulletproof vest. Their posture betrays their choice of rigidity and closure. People detect in them a certain standoffishness, as if they lived on a pedestal aloof from all pain or pleasure. This may be the last impression singles want to make and so they go to the opposite extreme, trying to turn even casual conversations into intimate encounters. Neither alienation nor fusion can solve the problem of secondary loneliness. It can only be resolved when we reach beyond our self-preoccupation to others.

Single life offers countless opportunities for respectful, helping encounters. We are less likely to feel lonely when we are with other persons, giving that extra inch or mile. These moments of befriending pull us out of the trap of self-pity. Being present to others, stopping to listen to their troubles, complimenting them for being thoughtful or accomplishing their task well—such outgoing acts enable us to transcend the loneliness of single living and to grow in the art of befriending others with the kind of love that finds its source in God.

Whenever I find myself becoming harsh, rigid, full of complaints and uncharitable, I know I am harboring a negative spirit. Nothing is more harmful to singles than this spirit of negativity. It attracts to itself ill spirits, like hardness of heart, that may be etched into harsh facial lines; pettiness spilling over into cheap gossip; resentment that crops up in envy of another's creativity; lack of forgiveness that harbors feelings of displeasure toward another, to say nothing of maladies like pervasive fatigue, sickly self-pity and depressive moods. A black cloud hangs over such a single life and people rightly regard such a person as a killjoy.

This unloving spirit is always divisive. It thrives on gossip and gripes. Underneath all of this misery let us hope there is still a person longing for the peace and joy of Christ. He has the power to dispel this spirit of negativity, to soften the mask of harshness. He gives us the grace we need to prevail over evil and the darkness it breeds. Instead of ignoring others or stepping over or on them, with the Lord's help I may be able to open my heart to them in charity, compassion and friendship. These formative dispositions enable us to renew our intention to love God and neighbor while welcoming the daily detachment that will gradually purify our hearts and promote communion with Christ.

The art of befriending is not something we know about from the moment of birth. We must learn how to love as we live and grow. Little children are not initially concerned about the welfare of their parents but about the gratification of their own needs. This needy love is essential for survival, but as time passes it must be transcended. Human progress depends on the shift from ego-centered to other-centered love. This shift, exemplified by the Lord who died to save us, is the goal of single loving. It includes my desire to receive love as well as to give it throughout life.

If we want a vivid illustration of what it means to love warmly yet freely, we can meditate on the life of Jesus. As a single person, He had about Him an ease, graciousness and affection that could draw all hearts. He touched responsive chords in whoever met Him, sharing with them wonder and joy as well as grief and weariness. He could thrill to the appeal of nature and be delighted by the innocence of a child.

As witnesses to the art of Christlike loving, we must not reduce singleness to some type of disembodied existence. We love as full-blooded, enfleshed men and women who run the risk of loving as Christ did. He does not want us to develop a counterfeit love of formal politeness, impersonal tolerance or vague humanitarianism. We need to root our loving in the earthy reality of our humanness while struggling to imitate the example of the Lord. Like Christ, we must listen first to the will of God speaking in the deepest recesses of our hearts and, out of this listening, hear and respond to the pleas of His people. Then we find the fulfillment that comes from being disciples who live in joyful obedience to His Word:

> *This is my commandment:*
> *love one another,*
> *as I have loved you.*
> *A man can have no greater love*
> *than to lay down his life for his friends.*

You are my friends,
if you do what I command you.
I shall not call you servants any more,
because a servant does not know
his master's business;
I call you friends,
because I have made known to you
everything I have learned from my Father.
You did not choose me,
no, I chose you;
and I commissioned you
to go out and to bear fruit,
fruit that will last;
and then the Father will give you
anything you ask him in my name.
What I command you
is to love one another.

(*Jn. 15:12–17*)

Suggested Readings

Aelred of Rievaulx. *On Spiritual Friendship*. Washington, D.C.: Cistercian Publications, 1974.

A humanist and a Christian monk, Aelred advocated friendship on both the natural and the supernatural plane. He saw frankness and not flattery, generosity and not gain, patience in correction, and constancy in affection as the marks of true friendship. If a friend prays for another, the friendship will be extended to include Christ. According to Aelred, there is nothing more advantageous to seek in human affairs than friendship. From being a friend of man, a man becomes a friend of God.

Boros, Ladislaus. *Meeting God in Man*. Trans. William Glen-Doepel. Garden City, N.Y.: Doubleday, Image Books, 1971.

The key to holiness lies in the fullest possible development of one's own humanity. By presenting a fresh approach to traditional virtues, the author emphasizes that we reach God by meeting Him in our brothers and sisters. The model for this meeting is Christ, whose life on earth is the most perfect example of how to attain true holiness by knowing, loving and identifying with our fellow men and women.

Buber, Martin. *I and Thou.* Trans. Walter Kaufmann. New York: Charles Scribner's Sons, 1970.
The author, best known for his revival of hasidism, a mystical movement among East European Jewry in the eighteenth and nineteenth centuries, elaborates his dialogical, or "I-Thou," philosophy of the mutual interaction between God and man. All real living, Buber believes, occurs in meeting, and all relation centers in the Eternal Relation, the mystery of our communion with God.

Fromm, Erich. *The Art of Loving.* New York: A Bantam Book, 1963.
Drawing upon his extensive experience in practice and teaching, Fromm validates his thesis that love is the only satisfactory answer to the problem of human existence. He shows why many are unable to develop their capacities for love due to a lack of maturity, self-knowledge and courage. Learning to love, like other arts, demands practice, concentration, insight and understanding. In this book, Fromm discusses not only romantic love and some false conceptions surrounding it but also love of parents for children; brotherly love; erotic love; self-love; and love of God.

Leech, Kenneth. *Soul Friend: The Practice of Christian Spirituality.* San Francisco: Harper & Row, 1977.
This text examines the concept of spiritual guidance in the Christian tradition from the Desert Fathers to the more recent thinking of the Roman Catholic Church, relating it to the contemporary quest for spirituality. Drawing on the teaching of the great spiritual guides, the text attempts to provide nourishment for the ministry of spiritual direction. A compendium of resources, it serves to introduce many people to the rich and diverse world of Christian spirituality.

Lotz, J. B. *The Problem of Loneliness.* New York: Alba House, 1967.
In our progress through history, we are accompanied by certain basic experiences in which the lines of our existence converge. Among these, loneliness takes a prominent place, for it is known to every epoch and is experienced by every human being. This experience springs from that common experience of humanity which remains constant throughout all the fluctuations of history

and which forms the inmost kernel, the ultimate depth of each person's own being. Lotz attempts in this book to liberate the voice of solitude from the dumbness imposed on it by isolation and so allow it to express itself. We must first come to grips with our isolation. Only then can we turn from the isolation that distorts us to the solitude that forms us.

Merton, Thomas. *No Man Is an Island.* New York: Harcourt, Brace, Jovanovich, 1978.

These sixteen meditations, written by one of the leading spiritual writers of our times, present his reflections on several foundational aspects of the spiritual life: love, hope, sincerity, conscience, prayer, vocation and solitude. Each of these traditional guiding values of Christian living offers the reader new hope amid the turmoil and challenge of our world, a promise that the peace and inner calm we desire is still possible today.

Muto, Susan Annette. *Renewed at Each Awakening: The Formative Power of Sacred Words.* Denville, N.J.: Dimension Books, 1979.

This work studies the power of sacred words to fashion our lives in relation to self, others and God. Part One contains reflections that emerged from living contact with the words of Scripture and the spiritual masters. Part Two deals specifically with spiritual reading as a formative art.

Squire, Aelred. *Summer in the Seed.* New York: Paulist Press, 1980.

This is a far-reaching reflection on the cultural situation of the modern believing and praying Christian seeking to nurture the seed of wisdom planted by writers and thinkers in our immediate past. Without neglecting the voices from our distant past, the author presents the related doctrines of incarnation and deification in the context of modern views of the human condition. Of special interest is his chapter on "Soul-Keepers."

Teresa of Avila. *The Way of Perfection.* Garden City, N.Y.: Doubleday, Image Books, 1964.

The most easily understood of her writings, *The Way of Perfection* is a practical guide to prayer which sets forth the saint's directives for the attainment of spiritual perfection. Three essentials of the prayer-filled life—fraternal love, detachment from created things, and true humility—are given special attention as the means to a lasting love of prayer and contemplation. This is a work of sublime beauty, bearing the mark of true spiritual genius.

van Kaam, Adrian. *Woman at the Well.* Denville, N.J.: Dimension Books, 1976.

Using the Gospel narrative of the meeting of Jesus with the Samaritan woman, the author explores and explicates both the art and discipline of meditative reading and our need to be receptive to the word of grace present at all moments in our everyday lives. Beginning with the implicit longing for liberation and fulfillment in the woman, the author traces her gradual transforming discovery of the hidden well of living water available to her through Christ.

——. "Provisional Glossary of the Terminology of the Science of Foundational Formation." *Studies in Formative Spirituality,* III, 2 (May 1982).

The author describes the process of social-presence depletion and presents terminology describing repletion sessions; formation conscience; dissonant social-presence; responsibility; and foundational compassion.

9

�֍✾✾✾✾✾✾✾✾✾✾✾✾✾✾✾
✾✾✾✾✾✾✾✾✾✾✾✾✾✾✾

Living Spiritually
as Single Persons
Within the Church

Listening to people talk about their experience, one often detects the theme that singles feel unrecognized by the Church. Many complain that there are ample programs for youth, for engaged and married adults, for the elderly, but little or nothing viable for career-oriented, committed singles, especially those between the ages of thirty-five and fifty-five. Those who have never been married may feel even more left out than the widowed, separated and divorced. They wonder what the Church is doing to help them in their human and Christian formation.

One could go on listing the areas of legitimate complaint, quoting impressive statistics and suggesting solutions to the predicament of singles in the Church, but this is not the approach I want to take. It seems more important to go behind the issues to a consideration of what it means experientially to live as a single person within the Church as it is presently structured. There is no use lamenting what was or wishing for what shall be. It seems more sensible to deal concretely with what is, first from the side of the single person, and then from the side of the Church as revealed in its Vatican Council II directives to the laity in the modern world.

SINGLES AND THE CHURCH

Of singles we would ask: What is the present quality and intensity of their spiritual life? In what way do they view their relationship to God and others? What is their attitude toward an always limited and limiting communal or parish situation? Do they add to the woes of a despairing, negating world or try to live in faith, hope and love? Do they behold the Formation Mystery revealing itself in limited persons, in priests, religious and fellow laity? Have they sufficiently explored the centrality of celibate love in the Church and attempted to foster this ideal? Do they see that out of solitude comes respectful sharing, that out of contemplative prayer comes openness to the world? Do they help people imagine the promise to come and thus encourage them to live hopefully in the limited present? Are they sources of resentment about *what is not*, or do they serve as reminders to the good that is there?

In short, in this matter of the relation between singles and the Church one could echo a familiar refrain, expressed like this: The first question is not, What can the Church do for me as a single person? but, What can I do for the Church? How can I as a single person live and witness to the foundations of Christian formation fostered generation after generation by the Church, such foundations as humility, forgiveness, reconciliation, love, peace and joy? What I must strive to change first is not outer structures but inner dispositions. Rather than asking what is wrong and why or how can it be changed, I need to explore my own attitudes.

For instance, an excellent disposition for singles to cultivate is generosity. If we miss out on chances to be generous, we miss out on the better part of our life within the Church. It happened recently that the pastor of my Church stopped me after Mass and asked if I would be interested in presenting a few talks during Lent for the parish. He obviously knew of my interest in formative spirituality. He hoped that as a single professional I could work these dates into my schedule. I felt happy to be able to say yes and thought to myself: "This will also be a good opportunity to share with others some reflections on spiritual formation and the single life." His invitation gave me a chance to exercise my single commitment to serve the Church. Frankly, I prefer this way of relating to that of waiting anxiously for the Church to devise programs for persons labeled SINGLE, as if this is a condition foreign to the rest of the population. In fact, singleness is the one common trait that binds us together.

Being generous is one way of serving the Church. Being gracious is another. By this I mean that singles ought to remind others of the mystery of God's gracious love at work in their lives. People in general seem starved for affirmation and nondemanding affection. Who better than single persons can become agents of benediction? It takes so little effort to compliment a fellow parishioner, to smile at a handicapped person, to radiate a peace that comes from within one's own prayerful presence to the Lord. This way of gracious response enables us to *be* Church within the Church.

The Church is not an institution in the abstract sense. It is the laity, the people of God, whom He calls to wholeness and holiness. Is He asking us as singles to help heal the split between the head and the heart, between abstract speculation about what the Church should be and do and the lived reality of what it is? It is a gathering of people around the Lord who loves us and wants us to be happy.

Prejudices that cut people off from their Common Source, attitudes that repress human dignity and freedom, negative sloganizing that produces more splits—these are the wounds that draw single people to the ministry of healing. Is not our call within the Church to help people move from disillusionment to an enlightened acceptance of the foundational directives that make us a Gospel people, reborn in spirit and truth?

To be single within the Church is to witness in a profound way to the uniqueness component or the celibate aspect of Christian life. This component is not only the center stone of celibate loving; it is as well a foundational aspect of Christian marriage. Couples who share their understanding of marriage as a sacrament and who want to talk about the growth of their relationship affirm that their marriage benefits from a wise rhythm of conjugal and celibate loving, of being intimately together and of respecting each other's solitude and uniqueness.

By witnessing to the celibate component, by loving celibately, single persons offer the Church a much needed service. They stand for the spiritual love that binds the Church to its people. They remind married couples of the sacredness of their pledge, of the transcendent bonds that preserve their loving union when the honeymoon is over, when their children leave home, when they must face life without one another due to disease or death.

Singles also serve the inwardness aspect of Christian living, an aspect often neglected in our socially conscious apostolic activities. They realize that people cannot hope to achieve publicly what they have not attained experientially within the inner boundaries of prayer. To be instruments of needed reformation of social structures, we have to expose ourselves consciously to the inner work of ongoing formation, of appraisal and reappraisal of our calling to serve the kingdom in either a hidden or public way.

From my experience at various conferences and conventions, I've found that many Christians hunger for spiritual leaders who can address deeper issues pertaining to our relation with the Lord. Many display expertise as planners and program chairpersons. Still other experts emerge who have evolved techniques guaranteed to stimulate communication, to enhance liturgical celebrations, to reveal ever more creative uses of audiovisual aids. Yet people remain spiritually hungry. Committees and Xeroxed outlines cannot fill this need. People are still dissatisfied, alienated, frustrated. They wonder where the Church is going and why their hearts are so seldom touched, despite these well-meaning efforts to create better parish communities and programs.

Perhaps single persons can provide the missing ingredient by their quiet, creative, thoughtful and prayerful spirit. Instead of concentrating solely on demonstrable objectives, they can remind fellow Church-goers of the invisible, imponderable, forming truths of spiritual living. By immersing themselves in the richness of the Christian formation tradition, they may remind others of the Forming Mystery at work in all members of the Church. They may become leaders in the truest sense, attracting others to God by their depth and personal holiness.

Within the Church singles can turn for inspiration to the example of those early Christians who lived single lives in the midst of the pagan Roman Empire as virgins and ascetics. Their choice of this way of witness was lauded as a means to keep alive the sense of the Sacred. They reminded others that God alone could fulfill the longing heart. Single Christians, living a spiritual life in today's world, may look to these early Christians for answers to the riddle of their life. They seem to confirm that superficial solutions are unsatisfactory, that lasting change must first take place in the hermitage of the heart.

Singles within the Church can bring to light hidden values related to the universal quest for holiness. They can help people realize anew neglected or forgotten dimensions of their relations with others and God. In their singleness they hold up a mirror in which the Church can see itself as the guardian of the Christian formation wisdom that can help us to become uniquely who we are.

A single friend of mine put it this way:

Look, I'm hardly the cheerleader type. You know that from your own experience. It's taken a while to really own and treasure this vocation. So what do I represent in the Church? Not its youth—by which I understand these spurts of new programs for singles —but its maturity, in the sense of having become a person who accepts the limits of reality and works within them to foster holiness.

In my eyes this friend aims as a single Christian to create fresh hope in a despairing world. He believes in making arid fields fertile again. In many ways he seeks to awaken in others the dormant values of spiritual living—all of this in a most hidden, ordinary way. His professional life as a teacher makes the usual demands upon him. But he is never so busy that he can't offer a kind word to others or listen to a friend. When something happens to rekindle my frustration about not being understood, I know I can go to him to renew my hope and joy. I've often thought that what we need in the Church is not more programs for singles but more single persons like him.

THE CHURCH AND SINGLES

In the Vatican Council II document, the Dogmatic Constitution on the Church, it is clearly stated in Chapter V and elsewhere that all the faithful, whatever their condition or state of life, are called by the Lord—each in his or her own way—to holiness according to the hidden plan of God.[1] As singles in the Church, it seems imperative that we hear and heed this universal call to holiness lived out uniquely by each person.

One additional service we can give the Church is to correct in every possible way the pre-Vatican II mentality that tended to identify holiness or spirituality as the special province of priests, brothers and sisters. It was as if the laity could lead good, moral, devotional lives but not aspire to a deeper spiritual life.

[1] *Lumen Gentium* (Dogmatic Constitution on the Church) in *The Sixteen Documents of Vatican II*, comp. J. L. Gonzales, S.S.P., and The Daughters of St. Paul (Boston: St. Paul Editions/Magister Books, 1965), pp. 109–90. See especially Chapter V, "The Universal Call to Holiness in the Church," pp. 151–57.

Among the laity married people were called by sacrament to a kind of conjugal holiness, but, alas, single persons had to struggle almost by default to find God. What a breath of fresh air Vatican II has been for us. It teaches that to live a spiritual life is basic for all Christians. Whether ordained, vowed, married or single, we need to experience intimacy with the Lord. Life empties out if we do not foster a living relationship with God. Who knows this better than single persons?

In the same document, *Lumen Gentium,* there is an interesting description of the Church as the building of God, based on the Lord's comparison of Himself to the stone the builders rejected but which was made the cornerstone of the entire edifice. In the same House of God dwells his family—teachers, firemen, social workers, lawyers, medical doctors, librarians, secretaries—each invited to share uniquely in the holiness of Christ, the cornerstone. The House of God is, therefore, a holy temple, a dwelling place of God among His people, that receives its durability from His perfection.[2]

What do the terms *building, family* and *temple* mean in the context of a formative spirituality for singles? Life is sometimes compared to a building, since it unfolds layer by layer upon a mysterious divine foundation. In this sense the Church as a building is a symbol of life. It contains all the pain and pathos, all the joy and playful abandonment that constitute the formation journey from birth to death. The Church values the presence of single persons who, like Jesus, become sensitive listeners to life in its ambiguity and clarity. Just as good solid buildings are composed of strong, single bricks, so the Church is a collection of unique members welded together by fidelity and love. It is a goal of single living within the Church that one become a strong component of the entire edifice, an inspiring presence wherever one is in the culture, thus drawing others to the Lord.

Singles value immensely the image of the Church as the family of God. It is important to sense that one belongs to this

[2] Ibid., p. 113.

family no matter where one lives or works. The Church helps
singles to meditate upon the mystery of participation in the
Body of Christ. Singles in turn help the Church by celebrating the diversity of gifts that enrich the unity of belonging to one and the same Body, to one and the same family.
This rhythm of uniqueness and unity is celebrated within the
Eucharistic Liturgy, where as unique members of one family
we all partake of the Body of Christ, knowing that if two or
three of us gather in His name, He is there in the midst of us.

Concretely, this family spirit may mean that the Church
feels responsible to uphold the single vocation before young
people as a viable option—as promising as the vocations to
marital, clerical or conventual life. It may mean that parishes
offer singles a chance to gather as a group for spiritual reading, scripture study, meditation and prayer, that they help
singles deepen their relationship with the Lord by supportive
formation programs.

Perhaps the proclamation of the Word in homilies can be
addressed to all adults and not just to families raising children. Once or twice a month, special liturgies could be
planned for single persons, followed by a social gathering that
promotes their career and cultural interests, that encourages
them to bring up for discussion such issues as housing needs,
the integration of spiritual life and secular commitments, the
quest for ways to make singles a more visible entity within
the Church.

Singles admit to the need for help and guidance from the
Church in such areas as sexuality; dealing with intimacy
while staying celibate; living alone or with aging parents;
communicating their vocation verbally or nonverbally. They
want to feel affirmed, welcomed, celebrated in the Church.
They consider themselves called by God to be a generous segment of His people, with many resources to offer, with a
wealth of talents and gifts. But they need a formative atmosphere in which to draw forth these gifts in a way that wipes
out stereotypes of the Sunday envelope-stuffer and explores
new avenues of service and ministry.

It would be tragic if the Church discouraged these single adults and continued to lose them either to other spiritual movements or to the pursuit of a godless secularism. Many singles seek guidance, but they are not satisfied with a scattering of partial answers and spiritual promises. They desire a unified approach to spiritual formation and a more meaningful inroad to participation in the life of the Church. Like it or not, they often feel excluded from the Church in whose family life they want to be included more than ever.

The imagery of temple, both in the sense of a sacred building and in the inner sense of each one's being the dwelling place of God, is also significant to single spirituality. The Church is the place to which we go to nurture our spiritual life as well as the place from which we go forth as Christ's disciples into the world. If we are to avoid the depletion of our spiritual presence, it is necessary to develop an inner life of contemplation. To contemplate means, literally, to be in the temple, that is, to seek that kingdom within, where God dwells lovingly beckoning each person to Himself.

Singles serve the Church by becoming contemplatives in the world. This means that they live in the awareness of God and that His presence does make a difference in their daily actions and decisions. God for them is not an abstraction but a living person. He is Brother, Friend, Father, Mother, Lover. As we open our hearts to His word, He responds to our needs in ways beyond imagining.

Thus, single spirituality within the Church is built on the cornerstone who is Christ. He is the foundation and center of our celibate lives. This spirituality is familial in that it provides the answer to our need to belong to a body of people whose covenant with God spans the ages. It is contemplative, meaning that we seek to become increasingly present to God in the midst of daily professional enterprises. We desire to deepen our personal relation with the Lord who loves us and invites us to remind others of His goodness. Thus, as singles we must not be content to sit passively in Church, waiting for others to make plans to assure our happiness. We are to take up actively these Vatican II directives and, above all, to deepen our spirituality.

In *Lumen Gentium* we read:

> *All members ought to be molded in the likeness of Him, until Christ be formed in them. For this reason we, who have been made to conform with Him, who have died with Him and risen with Him, are taken up into the mysteries of His life, until we will reign together with Him. On earth, still as pilgrims in a strange land, tracing in trial and in oppression the paths He trod, we are made one with His sufferings like the body is one with the Head, suffering with Him, that with Him we may be glorified.*[3]

In this text, as in so many others, we find the directives we need to live a fuller spiritual life within the Church. As single persons, it is important to see again that foundational Christian formation begins with the lived awareness that we are made in the image and form of God. He made us in His likeness and saw that all He made was good. Though since the Fall we have an inclination to sin due to pride, there is in us as well the longing to be conformed to Him and transformed by Him. How do we respond as singles to this call to transformation of heart?

One answer lies in taking upon ourselves in a personal way the mysteries of His life. As singles I believe that we are drawn in a special way to the hidden life of Jesus in Nazareth; to his preparation in the desert prior to His public mission; to His lonely nights spent in prayer before the Father; to His acceptance of the Father's will no matter what the personal cost; to His compassion for all human suffering. It is in the imitation and deepening of these Christlike attitudes that we will find our place as singles in the Church.

It is true, as I and my single friends have found out, that the more we grow in oneness with the Lord, the more we experience our pilgrim state. In quieter moments single persons will often share this feeling of being in a permanent state of

[3] Ibid., p. 115.

exile, that is, of feeling at home in the world but also of being conscious of a calling coming from beyond this earthly life. They will sometimes use the phrase "being amphibious creatures"—living with one foot in the temporal and another in the eternal. From my own experience I would have to agree. The more one tries to live in the presence of God, aware of the mystery of singleness, the more one experiences the loneliness and loveliness of the pilgrim state. I've used the following phrases in different journals to try to describe what I mean:

It's like being on the way to a new life while being commissioned to fully embrace the here and now reality with its joys and pains.

It's like traveling lightly so as not to be overly burdened with doubts, insecurities, fears. Journey's end is but a new beginning.

It's like sensing that one is carried by a forming mystery from birth, through life, into death and beyond to a new life of glory.

Clearly such a vocation entails an ongoing reflection on one's calling as single. At times this sense of the More Than requires that we assess our direction and make some changes in the vital or functional sphere. Always one is enthralled by the reality of the Transcendent and the truth that each dimension of life must serve the whole Mystery. It may thus become clear to singles within the Church that the Lord was probably asking us in a special way to become light on the mountain, leaven in the dough, salt of the earth.[4]

Wherever we are, in whatever role he places us, we need to cooperate with Him to bring the entire creation under one Head.

So you are no longer aliens or foreign visitors: you are citizens like all the saints, and part of God's

[4] See Mt. 5:13–16 and Mt. 13:33.

household. You are part of a building that has the apostles and prophets for its foundations, and Christ Jesus himself for its main cornerstone. As every structure is aligned on him, all grow into one holy temple in the Lord; and you too, in him, are being built into a house where God lives, in the Spirit.

(Ep. 2:19–22)

Jesus asks us to be Church within the world. As single Christians we are to seek the kingdom of God by participating enthusiastically in our careers, on this condition: that we order them according to the plan of God, seeking not our own honor and glory but His. We know that the web of our existence is woven from the ordinary circumstances of social and professional life. It is there that we seek our salvation, not on mountaintops isolated from the world. Ours is not the call of strict contemplatives, whose charism is also deeply needed by the Church. Our call is to be contemplatives in the world, sanctifying it from within as a leaven. In this quiet, hidden way we make Christ known to others—less by what we say or do as such and more by the testimony of a life resplendent in faith, hope and love, in respect for uniqueness and compassion for the human community.[5]

Let us, therefore, as singles take up the responsibility of building the Body of Christ in this post-Vatican Church and world. Though radiating a remarkable variety of gifts, we can rest in the unified peace of our love for the Lord. In this way we shall respond to the commission to make the Church known in the world not just as a place to gather socially but as a center of spiritual formation, helping its people to become the salt of the earth.

If programs are inaugurated, let them be devoted mainly to fostering the life of the spirit. This is what singles want most from the Church—not pious dating services but help with their spiritual life. They want to know how as single persons they can consecrate the world itself to the Lord. The key

[5] See *Lumen Gentium*, Chapter IV, "The Laity," p. 143.

question is: How can we as singles, in our work and prayer, in our creative endeavors and leisure hours, in our failures and successes, grow closer to the Spirit of the Lord and fulfill our divinely ordained call to a solitary spirituality in the world? I trust that this formative reflection on singles in the Church offers at least a partial answer.

Suggested Readings

Bloom, Anthony; and LeFebvre, Georges. *Courage to Pray.* New York: Paulist Press, 1973.
An exploration of prayer as encounter, inner freedom and being, by two men of prayer: as encounter, because through it we meet God, neighbor and ourselves, shorn of all pride and pretext; as inner freedom, for it must be approached without prejudice, humbly, sometimes cautiously, but always with courage; as being, for it is not something added on but a being aware of what we are. "It is and remains our deepest truth even when we walk in darkness."

De Foucauld, Charles. *Meditations of a Hermit.* Trans. Charlotte Balfour. New York: Orbis Books, 1981.
Although Brother Charles was no academic theologian, his experience and love of the cross, his unceasing search after the will of God and his complete self-effacement in solitude with the Lord brand him as an authentic theologian in the traditional sense of being a "saint-theologian." The letters, meditations and spiritual direction in his volume enable the reader to follow the humble, but influential, religious in his journey, first as a Trappist at Notre Dame des Nieges and Akbes, then as a servant of the Poor Clares at Nazareth, and finally as a hermit and priest at Beni-Abbes and in the Hoggar.

Lumen Gentium (Dogmatic Constitution on the Church). *The Sixteen Documents of Vatican II.* Comp. J. L. Gonzales, S.S.P., and The Daughters of St. Paul. Boston: St. Paul Editions/Magister Books, 1965, 109–90.
This important Council document contains chapters on the mystery of the Church; the people of God; the Church's hierarchical structure; the laity; the universal call to holiness in the Church; religious life; the eschatological nature of the pil-

grim Church and its union with the Church in heaven; and the Blessed Virgin Mary in the mystery of the Church. This document stresses that the Church is a mystic reality, steeped in the presence of God. To read it prayerfully is to gain new and deeper insights into the Church's teaching about herself.

Nouwen, Henri. *The Wounded Healer: Ministry in Contemporary Society.* Garden City, N.Y.: Doubleday, Image Books, 1979.

What does it mean to be a minister in contemporary society? This question has been raised during the last few years by many men and women who want to be of service but find the familiar ways crumbling. In this book the author proposes a far-reaching approach to making those familiar ways more effective and relevant in our fragmented culture. Noting that modern humans are above all suffering humans, wounded as they are by lack of hope, by loneliness, by the predicament of rootlessness, ministers today can only help others deal with these problems if they are willing to go beyond their professional role and leave themselves open as fellow human beings with their own wounds and suffering. Nouwen suggests concrete methods by which ministers can use this creative human dialogue to bring freedom and liberation to those afflicted by the major anxieties of our times. He considers finally how this personal interformative relationship will affect the lives of the ministers themsleves, these lonely men and women wounded so they can help others.

Rite of Christian Initiation of Adults (Ordo Initiationis Christianae Adultorum). Washington, D.C.: USCC Publications Office, 1974.

The new *Rite of Christian Initiation of Adults* sets before the Church in a clear and normative way the successive stages in the process of living under the mystery of Christ's dying and rising continuously among his faithful. It presents and celebrates a style of life suffused with a graced, concrete commitment, of both body and soul, to Christ's real presence in the Church and in the world. It proclaims Christ's passover, here and now, as an unbounded, ongoing reality restoring all life in His life, the gift of God's merciful love.

"Spiritual Formation and Family Life." *Studies in Formative Spirituality.* II, 3 (November 1981).

Responding to the widely accepted perception that the contemporary family is facing a serious crisis, the *Institute of Formative Spirituality* has devoted an entire issue of *Studies* to exploring and revitalizing the foundational components of the spiritual formation of the family. Timely articles on fundamental spiritual, theological, and formative approaches to the critical value of family life seek to restore the depth and promise of living in God's vision of the world as family.

Squire, Aelred. *Asking the Fathers: The Art of Meditation and Prayer*. New York: Paulist Press, 1973.
This text traces the main lines of the teachings of the saints and mystics throughout Christian history. More than an anthology, it aims to present the various parts of Christian teaching as an interconnected whole. The practice of prayer and meditation is placed within the context of an overall view of life that is consistent with the foundational formative traditions of the Church.

van Kaam, Adrian. *The Vowed Life*. Denville, N.J.: Dimension Books, 1968.
The theme of the "threefold path" of obedience, respectful love and poverty of spirit is traced from its anthropological and biological roots to its meaning for commitment and consecration to a lasting life-style. The dynamics of life call and the healing power of the vows are developed alongside the obstacles to religious living in Western culture. A mere service approach to involvement in our utilitarian culture contrasts with the author's emphasis on the implicit and explicit value of fully religious participation in our world.

——. *Looking for Jesus*. Denville, N.J.: Dimension Books, 1978.
A practical and prayerful approach to Scripture reading as illustrated through the use of the Last Discourse of Jesus. Each chapter serves as a reflection on a passage from the Discourse and shows the reader how to derive spiritual truths and insights from his or her own reading of Scripture. The Epilogue provides guidance for those interested in the art and discipline of formative Scripture reading.

——. "Provisional Glossary of the Terminology of the Science of Foundational Formation." *Studies in Formative Spirituality*, III, 3 (November 1982).
In this glossary the author describes the process of interformation and the essential dispositions necessary for wholesome human and Christian formation.

10

✣✣✣✣✣✣✣✣✣✣✣✣✣✣✣✣✣✣
✣✣✣✣✣✣✣✣✣✣✣✣✣✣✣✣✣

Expressing Singleness in Word, Action and Style of Life

What does singleness have to say in a world where marriages crumble, where human life is treated like a useless commodity, where violence makes people fear walking in the streets or ever trusting strangers? This style of life, lived spiritually, inevitably contradicts selfish relating, man-centered ideologies and evil uses of power. Singles are committed to values that reverence life and respect uniqueness. Theirs is a love that responds to the cry for a healing touch in a wounded world by exercising compassion—a love that gives before it takes, that holds on but also lets go.

Single-hearted love seems to release in others whatever it is that blocks the flow of formation, including unfaithfulness, dehumanization and senseless violence. The challenge is to touch persons in their uniqueness without crushing them. We can suggest five conditions that facilitate this expression of single loving in word, action and style of life.

Because singles like to see themselves as members of God's family, they attend to the call repeated throughout Scripture and the formation tradition to treat others as we would have them treat us. This directive leads us not only to give others their due in justice but also to go one step further and reach them in mercy and kindness.

Secondly, we try to make these formation ideals concrete in some form of loving action according to what each situation requires. In some cases what may be needed is monetary help, but more often than not we express kindness in gentle support of another's endeavors, in a quiet smile of reassurance, in a word of forgiveness.

Thirdly, it is as important that we learn to receive graciously the acts of kindness that others show us. People will soon be put off by a tough "I don't need your help" attitude. It is potentially deformative to pull back out of a false sense of independence. To be a helper of others means learning to accept help from them.

Fourthly, growth in singlehearted loving ought to evoke a noticeable increase in sensitivity to the real needs of others. We may develop a kind of "sixth sense" or prereflexive recognition of how to read the heart of another. A really wounded person may need double doses of compassion, while another who is clearly taking advantage of our generosity may need the "tough love" treatment.

Finally, the way we express our love must reflect our capacity to see Christ in another person, whether that person appears in a business suit or a beggar's robe. It is up to us to appraise whether the problem is one of abandonment of soul or abandonment of body. Again, the help we offer has to be given in accordance with the just demands of our situation and of our God-given capacities to serve one or another segment of the population. As singles, we must resist the deceptive posture of trying to be all things to all people. No matter what segment we serve, Christ is there. He can use us to express His love, if we let Him.

Understood spiritually, to be single is a sign of the basic incompleteness of this life. To live this vocation is to remind others that no human love can fulfill us totally. There is more that the human heart seeks, and this More is God. I remember thinking after I read *Showings* by the English mystic Julian of Norwich, anchoress and spiritual directress: Julian seems to say that the greatest honor I can give to God is to live joyfully because of the knowledge of His love. Single lovers, therefore, resist any ploys to place persons under their control. Instead, by loving others in imitation of Christ's attitudes and actions, they offer them a glimpse in this life of the love we shall experience in eternity.

INTEGRATING FUNCTIONALITY AND SPIRITUALITY

As an expression of their vocation, single persons must try to become masters in the art of combining the functional and the spiritual. As an artist blends two colors to form one rich hue, so we must labor hard to accomplish our goals while making these subservient to the will of God. We must remind ourselves and others that the gifts we have are given to us by God, lest we become addicted to achievement and acquisition. Our approach to functioning has to be one of open hands, not clenched fists.

To understand more fully this problem of integrating the functional and the transcendent in word and action, it might help if we ponder the meaning of success and failure from a faith perspective. At one time I served as public relations director of a fund-raising campaign for a charitable organization. I was asked to plan the approach we would use to reach the public, complete with promotional aids, display advertising and media contacts. I had a few weeks to work on the project prior to presenting my ideas and plans to the Board of Directors. Intense work yielded what I thought was the ideal way to go, based admittedly on limited experience. I can still taste the bitter flavor of failure when the Board rejected my plans and coolly told me to try again.

Later, as I sorted out my feelings, I realized I had learned a lot about failure. I found that failure is an experience that affects all levels of our life, and hence the quality of our expression and appearance. For instance, fatigue and failure go hand in hand, maybe because we put so much energy into having to succeed. I felt drained for days afterward. I doubted for a while my ability to function in that field.

Negative emotions surfaced heatedly—anger, irritability, resentment. These influenced in turn my spiritual life. It was especially difficult that day to calm myself and to pray without distracting memories of the meeting. I could have easily slipped into a vicious circle of introspection, replaying the scenario that led up to that failure and figuring out ways in which it could have been prevented "if only . . ."

Why did failure, which is perfectly human, lead to these bad feelings? Was it perhaps because as a single person I valued success too highly? After all, there was no spouse or children waiting at home to welcome and affirm me despite this small setback.

The question surfaced more strongly than ever: How can single persons cope with failure and success from a spiritual perspective? This honestly faced question alerted me to the realization that success, viewed from a transcendent perspective, can be a failure experience. If I never failed on the human level, I might forget the need for faith and begin to base my single vocation on evidence of worldly fame and success. Thus the rejection of my plans, a curse humanly speaking, became a blessing in disguise spiritually.

The ramifications of this discovery led to new insights regarding what constitutes a way of life ultimately lived only for God. For instance, good health, abounding energy, physical beauty—these are signs, so to speak, of bodily success. Such signs incline us to equate our worth with looking good, with making up and staging life so as to create an unforgettable impression. One can go so far as to make gratification everything. The clearest proof of one's being "with it" becomes performance in sex.

What happens, however, when life deals us the inescapable blows of aging, sickness, pending death—processes that cannot be halted no matter how much we idolize the body? Such vital failures happen whether we want them to or not. They remind us that we are temporal beings. Thus, bodily failure, when accepted gracefully, can facilitate spiritual awakening.

Something similar takes place on the level of functioning. Here success is measured by achievement, status, financial gain. Society insists that one be on the winning side. Since we tend to mock the losers of the world, singles who already feel unsure of themselves may try twice as hard to succeed. Before long, however, the resistances of life intervene.

Projects we counted on never come to conclusion. Business partners betray one another. Failure nips at our best-laid plans. Does not this same functional failure prompt us to reflect on our spiritual priorities? When will we learn that we are persons valued in God's eyes and not merely performance machines? He loves us for who we are, not just for what we do or fail to get done.

This shift to the transcendent perspective reveals the relative value of success or failure in God's eyes. This means that instead of seeing failure as a source of discouragement, we can view it as a stimulant to hope. Instead of making failure an occasion for self-chastisement, we can accept it in faith as an invitation to advance in spiritual awareness.

Destructive responses to failure include becoming defensive, blaming others, growing bitter. Constructive responses echo this familiar quotation adopted by many groups in addition to the members of Alcoholics Anonymous: "God, grant me the serenity to accept the things I cannot change, the courage to change the things I can, and the wisdom to know the difference."

EXPRESSING THE ESSENTIALS OF SINGLE SPIRITUAL LIVING

Following these inner transcendent directives may mean a departure from a current yet inauthentic way of life that arouses in me feelings of true spiritual guilt. In the light of these feelings, I have to grapple honestly with the presuppositions that have guided my single life up to now. Perhaps I have conformed more to worldly rather than to spiritual directives. I have not listened to the inner voice of the Lord and responded to my foundational life form. Is it too late, or can I still express this Christ form as a single person present to God in the world?

As I grow to accept more fully who I am in Christ, I am better able to separate the essentials of my calling from peripheral accretions. I may find that some of the things for which I've felt guilty are really not matters essential to the meaning and living of a single life but only imagined violations of culturally conditioned codes.

False guilt feelings arise at times from my fear of being different. This guilt of standing away from the crowd could be called "separation guilt." It is linked to my fear of being lonely, of feeling cut off from others for not following the popular style of doing things. Separation guilt is thus concerned with appearances. I try to look like I'm having a good time—which may be necessary out of compassion for my hostess. The problem arises when I try to convince myself that I am having a good time and feel guilty admitting that this party craze is not my cup of tea. The opposite extreme is just as bad: to pout in solitude and then go out piously to bestow my love on others. What matters is finding the right expression at the right time: thoroughly enjoying a good party and socializing affably; meeting a special friend and facing the joys and struggles of our relationship; stepping aside for a while in solitude.

Idealizing guilt is related to separation guilt and is equally as false. I may feel guilty, for example, when I have to say no to someone because this "no" seems out of keeping with the ideal picture I have of myself as always cooperative, thoughtful, generous and outgoing. But it is false to feel guilty about things that are impossible for me to be or do at this time. When my single life becomes an attempt to live up to the ideal me, I may be driven to act in ways untrue to the person I am. Maybe I'm not as charming as I would like to be, maybe my words do not always come out as I'd like. Why feel guilty about that?

If I further explore this guilt, I find that it is due less to the "no" I have to say than to the subtle remarks and uplifted eyebrows of others who—understandably conscious of their own needs—fail to consider mine. This guilt begins to diffuse with the discovery that I am more concerned about their and my own idealized image of the single life than with an acceptance of the limits of this vocation.

BEING REALISTIC
ABOUT SINGLENESS

As single persons, we must try to be realistic about life. Otherwise, lacking the toughening influence of spouses and children, we may remain adolescents living in a dream world where everything unfolds according to a self-satisfying scenario. Life simply does not work that way. It is never a matter of doing one's own thing, for life always unfolds within a limited situation. It is guided by given circumstances, though we are free to take an attitude toward these givens and appraise their directive power in regard to our personal formation.

We have to listen to our life history, to the limits of our vitality, to our functional talents and ambitions and, most of all, to transcendent aspirations and pneumatic inspirations. This listening within our here-and-now communal situation and the world at large makes us realistic. It is crucial to survival in the single state. Without careful, ongoing appraisal, we may fall into illusion and betray our vocation.

For the sober truth is that single persons often give in to cultural pressures. They feel obliged to have a lively social life. What would people think if they never had a date? If they preferred to stay home at night and read a book rather than "score"? How many singles feel compelled to marry even when they know inside that they ought to remain alone? How many have the courage to say no even to the right person and remain good friends?

A similar problem occurs in relation to one's job. Despite frequent signals of incompatibility, singles may refuse to change fields or seek further education because the security they've found holds them fast. Fear dominates their inner life, not freedom and love. Singles who are too insecure and complacent to admit failure in career choice may have to face a bitter, unfulfilled future. In all of these cases they have refused to listen to the foundations of their life formation—to the God-given graces of congeniality, compatibility and compassion.

Again we return to the key issue of accepting myself as I am, with no illusions and no idle comparisons. Humble acceptance of self is at the same time an act of courage, the courage to be who I am, no more and no less. Christ did not promise that such acceptance would be easy or without pain. He did promise to be with us always and to make us channels of His love in this world.

Lighthearted realism—that is crucial for single living. That, and the sense, as each day goes by, of the redeeming power of Christ's love that forgives me for the mistakes of the past, comforts me in the present and promises His fidelity in the future. With eyes of faith I see the will of God unfolding in my life in a mysterious way, even if I cannot account logically for every thread in the mosaic of His providence. Despite all setbacks, it becomes easier to utter these oft-quoted words of Dag Hammarskjöld:

> *For all that has been—thanks!*
> *To all that shall be—yes!*

With this attitude we are no longer content to undergo life passively but feel eager to cooperate with our calling creatively. Admittedly, present-day society is a confusion of paradigms and life-styles. Yet it also offers singles a greater variety of possibilities to grow as spirit-directed Christians, as dynamic professionals, as witnesses to the values all persons secretly desire.

To be faithful to our divine direction is not a static knowing but an ongoing quest. We only emerge by moving from our current life to the next stage, selecting and integrating changes we believe to be expressions of God's will for us. Real formation always involves this transition from the old to the new in a way that does not betray our foundational life form. We sense in faith where we ought to go and how we can get there in a way that respects the unique persons we are.

Instead of being carried along powerless and without reflection by the pace of the world, instead of following someone else's prescription for success, we can learn to participate in secular life selectively and in gratitude for our single vocation. In this way we can incarnate values that benefit society without loss of our unique direction or diminishment of our presence to the Eternal Love that carries us.

FUTURE DIRECTIONS FOR SINGLE SPIRITUAL LIVING

As we approach the twenty-first century, it makes sense to offer singles an alternative to the role models and living experiments that most of us are familiar with through the media, if not firsthand. The alternative does demand a certain surrender of egocentric ambitions and the need to be in control of one's own turf. This surrender to a guiding, forming Other does not imply complacency. Everything we've said points to the challenge of living a single, spiritual life. We must remain dynamic, esthetic, presentable, expressive, affectionate, reflective men and women. The only difference is that we do not seek status, power and possession for their own sake. What matters now is service to the Lord and remembrance of the values He represents. That means dedication, compassion and personal integrity.

Experience shows that efficiency and surrender to transcendent directives can go hand in hand. We become spontaneous, relaxed, gracious persons who can accomplish much in this world. What we strive for, in other words, is a union of full human presence and faith. We want at the end of our lives to be able to trace the directing line of God's love from childhood to adolescence to adulthood. We want to see His forming plan written in the pattern of our single life with its joys and pains, triumphs and trials, successes and failures, promises and problems.

We have no illusions that things will be perfect outside that final movement into the fullness of God's peace. Now is the time to unite human becoming and belief in God, to leave behind the wasteland of spiritual exhaustion and enter the land of spiritual regeneration. To capture what I mean, let me paraphrase a passage from T. S. Eliot's poem "Choruses from 'The Rock.'"

In the opening lines he addresses our condition in contemporary society. He suggests that though ours is an age of technical progress—after all we have mastered scientifically enough data to place men on the moon—ours may really be an age of spiritual regression.

He describes life today as an endless cycle of idea and action, endless invention, endless experiment. This age brings knowledge of motion but not of stillness; knowledge of speech but not of silence; knowledge of words and ignorance of the Word. All our knowledge, he says, brings us nearer to our ignorance; all our ignorance brings us nearer to death, but no nearer to God.

Then he asks the heartrending questions: Where is the life we have lost in living? Where is the wisdom we have lost in knowledge? Where is the knowledge we have lost in information? His conclusion is rather devastating: The cycles of heaven in twenty centuries bring us farther from God and nearer to the dust.

The poet's words jar us out of complacency. We too ask about the life we have lost in living, about the wisdom we have lost in our efforts to gather information, about the failure of communication in an era that has amassed so many techniques. What has happened to us and why? What part does the single person play in the work of restoration?

I believe it is up to single, believing persons everywhere to try to heal the artificial split between life and religion by living in word, action and style of expression the unity of a fully Christian formation. That is why we have stressed the significance in our lives of good reading, of abiding with the Word, of living in silence and solitude, of fostering foundational values.

In the Church today we need single men and women of profound spiritual depth who, out of the resources of their own interior life with the Lord, live as other Christs in the world and radiate that power to a population hungry for true Christian formation. Singles do have a mission in life to fulfill, a special yet foundational task fashioned for them by God. No matter how narrow or expansive their circumstances, no matter how limited or gifted their ability, they can and must radiate a meaning no other person can give to the world in present and future times.

Of course, it will be difficult. Single spiritual living was never meant to be easy. We need only to witness the agony of Christ to understand the pain we may have to endure. But we have a promise in which to believe. And, more than that, we have a Single Person who lived as one of us, who laid down His life for all of us.

Guided and inspired by the Spirit of the Lord, our lives as single persons can become models of peace, joy and integrity. People will behold in us a hope, a grace, a faith toward which they cannot help but feel an attraction. Our lives will become sources of formative benediction as we share with others the affirmation God has shown to us. Their well-being often depends on the way in which we show respect for their uniqueness. Let us not withhold this blessing. Let our singleness become a living witness to the integration of personal and social presence all people seek. We may not understand all that God asks, yet in faith and trust we can say yes to the vocation He has chosen for us. Then His peace will surpass our anxious concerns.

In conclusion, let me share with each person reading this book a prayer I wrote for myself and for all who live the single life as His messengers in the world:

Lord, I sometimes feel like a wind-tossed reed. The world's a stormy place. I'm hurt by lack of understanding. I become harsh with others and then try to whip myself and them into a perfect mold, forgetting your graced mystery of formation. Then I think of you and your disciples that night on the lake. You calmed their fears as you calmed the waters and reprimanded them for their lack of faith. You showed them what faith really means by walking on the water.

When I look at you, a certain peace comes over me. You have made me a unique person. My singleness is an unrepeatable offering of self through you to the world. In this moment of inwardness, I recognize anew the value of being who I am.

Below the troubles of my mind and the emotional upsurges, I descend into the spiritual center of my soul. I allow myself to slip down, to let go . . . knowing that in this sacred core and center I am held, sustained, embraced by an Infinite Peace.

Here, at the still point below all agitation, I am encompassed by you. In the peace of this moment, muscles relax; my mind is free of preoccupying thoughts; the whole of me is enveloped by your love. From this inner peace there flows a willingness to reach out to others in service, friendship and care.

*Nourished by your word, held by your love, help me
to become a message-bearer in the world, a humble
servant of the mystery of divine formation.*

Suggested Readings

Eliot, T. S. *Four Quartets.* New York: Harcourt, Brace & Company, Inc., A Harvest Book, 1943.

This poem in four movements is widely considered the culminating expression of Eliot's art. Throughout this work he recalls our fundamental quest for spiritual meaning amid the wasteland of twentieth-century culture. He echoes our irrepressible hope for transforming union with the Transcendent Mystery of our lives.

Julian of Norwich. *Showings.* Trans. Edmund Colledge, O.S.A. New York: Paulist Press, 1978.

Revelations given to an anchoress living in fourteenth-century England, these sixteen "showings" of God's love offer us a warm and simple reflection on the deepest mysteries of our share in His divine plan. Expressed in a langauge at once humorous and profound, perennial truths concerning sin, grace, redemption, the humanity of Christ, and the motherly mercy of God the Father are presented with a quiet humility by one who knew from experience that God dwells among us.

Kelly, Thomas R. *A Testament of Devotion.* New York: Harper & Row, Publishers, 1941.

Kelly's book is an ideal companion to that highest of all human arts, the lifelong conversation between God and his creatures. In the five essays of the Testament—"The Light Within," "Holy Obedience," "The Blessed Community," "The Eternal Now and Social Concern," "The Simplification of Life"—there emerges a clear-cut path through the underbrush of day-to-day worries and frustrations into the cool glades of spiritual peace. As a devotional text, it ranks among the few that are great and undying.

van Kaam, Adrian; and Muto, Susan. *Tell Me Who I Am.* Denville, N.J.: Dimension Books, 1977.

Many Christians today are searching for a personal, spiritual self-direction to help them cope with rapidly changing social values and life-styles. This text takes up many of the questions to which this search gives rise, such as life in community, self-acceptance, commitment, prayer, personal feelings, and religious formation. A well-balanced initiation into the art of spiritual self-direction, this book offers much to all who seek to serve the divine mystery of our formation revealed in the context of their unique personal lives.

——. *Am I Living a Spiritual Life? Questions and Answers on Formative Spirituality.* Denville, N.J.: Dimension Books, 1978.

A series of questions and answers, in chapter form, designed to help readers get in touch with themselves and their life direction. Reflective meditations enable one to take distance from everyday preoccupations that can cloud one's vision and awareness of the Spirit's presence in daily life. The circumstances of everyday living are shown to be a chain of divine appeals wherein one can decipher God's will and learn to respond from the depths of one's being.

Weil, Simone. *Waiting for God.* New York: Harper & Row, Publishers, Harper Torchbooks, 1951.

This collection of letters and essays by a contemporary French philosopher gathers a portion of her religious writings under the theme of patient waiting on the revelation of life's ultimate meaning. Since her untimely death in 1943 at the age of thirty-four, Simone Weil has more and more become an exemplary witness to the mystery of our encounter with the Divine in everyday life. Her life and writings challenge the self-deceit and smugness of an "easy" faith with the uncomfortable reality and awful burden of God's self-sacrificing love.

Dr. Susan Annette Muto is Director of the Institute of Formative Spirituality and Managing Editor of its two journals, *Studies in Formative Spirituality* and *ENVOY*. A native of Pittsburgh, she completed her undergraduate degree at Duquesne University and her graduate studies in literature at the University of Pittsburgh.

After a brief career in journalism and public relations, she became Assistant Director of the Institute in 1965, a position that changed the direction of her life and led her into her present dedication to teaching, speaking, writing and research in the field of foundational formation.

As a single laywoman, living her vocation in the world, and supported by over eighteen years of experience in the Institute, Dr. Muto is more than qualified to address the formation concerns of laity, clergy and religious. In addition to her administrative and academic responsibilities as a professor in the Institute's master's and doctoral programs, Dr. Muto is a prolific author and a renowned speaker, both nationally and internationally.

Dr. Muto is the eldest of three children. Her parents live in the Pittsburgh vicinity, as do her two brothers and their families. She enjoys traveling, attending theater productions, art shows, and the symphony. Her time is also spent in doing what she loves most—reading and writing within the framework of the Christian formation tradition, especially as it is recorded in the writings of both pre- and post-Reformation spiritual masters.

This book tells in part her own story and intends to respond to the formation questions of all single people.